Boston

Buffalo

Bethlehem

New York City

Cleveland

Philadelphia

Pittsburgh

X & FOX

Ohio River

Cincinnati

Vincennes

St. Louis

Louisville

New Harmony

ippi River

New Orleans

VIEWS OF A

VANISHING

FRONTIER

VIEWS OF A
VANISHING
FRONTIER

John C. Ewers

Marsha V. Gallagher
David C. Hunt
Joseph C. Porter

Published by the Center for Western Studies/Joslyn Art Museum, Omaha,
Nebraska and distributed by University of Nebraska Press, Lincoln-London
Made possible by InterNorth, Inc.

4

Library of Congress Cataloging
in Publication Data

Ewers, John C.
  Views of a vanishing frontier.

  Catalogue of an exhibition which originated at the
Joslyn Art Museum and which will travel to the
Amon Carter Museum, Fort Worth, Texas; Fine Arts
Museums of San Francisco, M. H. de Young
Memorial Museum, San Francisco, California;
National Museum of Natural History/Smithsonian
Institution, Washington, D.C.; and The Metropolitan
Museum of Art, New York, New York (Karl Bodmer
watercolors only).
  Includes bibliographical references.
  1. Indians of North America—Missouri River
Valley—Exhibitions. 2. Missouri River Valley—
Description and travel—Exhibitions. 3. Bodmer, Karl,
1809-1893—Exhibitions. 4. Maximilian, Prince of
Wied-Neuwied—Exhibitions. I. Ewers, John Canfield.
II. Joslyn Art Museum
E78.M82V54 1984   978.02   83-25558
ISBN 0-936364-12-2 Hard Cover
ISBN 0-936364-13-0 Soft Cover

This exhibition is made possible by InterNorth, Inc.

Exhibition Schedule

Joslyn Art Museum, Omaha, Nebraska
February 12 to April 8, 1984

Amon Carter Museum, Fort Worth, Texas
May 19 to July 29, 1984

Fine Arts Museums of San Francisco, M. H. de Young
Memorial Museum, San Francisco, California
September 8 to November 18, 1984

National Museum of Natural History/Smithsonian
Institution, Washington, D.C.
January 4 to March 31, 1985

The Metropolitan Museum of Art, New York, New York
July 17 to October 6, 1985
(Karl Bodmer watercolors only)

Published by
Center for Western Studies, Joslyn Art Museum
2200 Dodge St.
Omaha, Nebraska 68102-1292
402-342-3300

Distributed by
University of Nebraska Press
Lincoln, Nebraska and London, England

Cover: Karl Bodmer
Wahktägeli (Gallant Warrior), Yankton Sioux Chief
Watercolor on paper
The InterNorth Art Foundation/Joslyn Art Museum

Frontispiece: Plate 2. *Travellers Meeting with Minatarre [Hidatsa] Indians*

Copy Editors: Theodore W. James and Ann E. Birney

Catalogue Designers: Julie and Lou Toffaletti, Montgomery, Alabama

Cover Design: Staples & Charles Ltd, Washington, D.C.

Exhibition Design: Staples & Charles Ltd, Washington, D.C.

Photography: Jay Johnson: 26; Linden-Museum, Stuttgart, photograph by
Ursula Didoni: 67; Lorran Meares: 6, 23, 29, 31, 40, 47, 51, 60, 68; Museum of the
American Indian, Heye Foundation: 17; National Anthropological Archives,
Smithsonian Institution: 15, 25, 33; National Museum of Man, National Museums of
Canada, Neg. #S75-449: 41; Staatliche Museen Preussischer Kulturbesitz, Museum für
Völkerkunde, Berlin, photograph by Gisela Oestreich: 62; Gary Swanson: 2, 36, 42, 44,
45, 46, 48, 50, 52, 54, 58, 64; The University Museum, University of Pennsylvania: 1;
Malcolm Varon ©Varon: 3, 4, 5, 7, 8, 9, 10, 11, 13, 14, 16, 18, 19, 20, 21, 22, 24, 27, 28, 30,
32, 34, 35, 37, 38, 39, 43, 49, 53, 55, 56, 57, 59, 61, 63, 65, 66, 69.

Map Graphic: Staples & Charles Ltd, Washington, D.C.

Composition: Compos-it, Inc., Montgomery, Alabama

Production & Lithography: Stephenson , Alexandria, Virginia

Contents

Foreword

It was a former chairman of the board of our corporation, John F. Merriam, now retired, who had the vision which led to our purchase in 1962 of the outstanding Maximilian-Bodmer collection. In the intervening years we have strived for a guardianship position which allowed for a mix of proper conservation efforts combined with limited public exposure. The latter primarily came in the form of selected, individual exhibitions in our corporation's various areas of operation. It may well be that the collection, which so richly recorded the customs and cultures of the native Americans along the upper Missouri, is not as universally well-known as it deserves to be.

With this in mind, the occasion of the sesquicentennial observation of Prince Maximilian's expedition is being utilized for the first major national tour of the collection. Indeed, it is our distinct privilege to sponsor this unique exhibition, organized by the Joslyn Art Museum, which takes the best of the exquisite works of Karl Bodmer and the valuable documents of Prince Maximilian and combines them with pertinent ethnographic material graciously loaned by a number of leading North American and European museums and institutions.

We hope that you will share in our conviction that *Views of a Vanishing Frontier* provides a rewarding reflection upon the priceless legacies represented in the exhibition and in this catalogue. It is our further hope that this sponsorship is a consistent extension of our corporation's continuing thematic expression, "We Work for America".

Sam F. Segnar
President and Chief Executive Officer
InterNorth, Inc.

Introduction

Commemorating the 150th anniversary of the expedition of German Prince Maximilian of Wied and Swiss artist Karl Bodmer to North America, the exhibition *Views of a Vanishing Frontier* visually recreates this historic journey into the early 19th century American wilderness which was on the brink of rapid and dramatic change.

Chronologically organized, the show depicts this epic journey utilizing Bodmer's watercolors combined with a selection of ethnographic and historic objects from museum collections in Europe and America. Along with Bodmer's watercolors, Maximilian's written accounts of the expedition chronicle the land and the people they encountered along the way. A selection of artifacts personally collected by Maximilian is included in the exhibition, some of which are also depicted in Bodmer's watercolors.

The expedition lasted two years, from July 4, 1832 to July 16, 1834. Upon his return to Germany, Maximilian published accounts of the journey in German, French and English. A picture atlas of eighty-one aquatints after Bodmer's watercolors illustrated these editions. Following these publications, Bodmer's original North American watercolors were deposited with Maximilian's manuscripts at the Wied family estate. Here they remained, unknown or forgotten, until rediscovered after World War II by a Koblenz museum director.

Bodmer's watercolors toured West Germany and the United States during the 1950s, after which the collection was sold to M. Knoedler and Company in New York in 1959. In 1962 InterNorth, Inc. purchased the collection and placed it on permanent loan at the Joslyn Art Museum in Omaha, Nebraska. *Views of a Vanishing Frontier* has been made possible by InterNorth, Inc.

Maximilian's extensive ethnographic and natural history collections were dispersed throughout North America and Europe before Bodmer's watercolors and Maximilian's related archival material were rediscovered. The Prince's significant collection of flora and fauna consisting of thousands of specimens was sold to the American Museum of Natural History in New York City in 1869. The North American Indian artifacts collected by Maximilian survive today principally at the Linden-Museum in Stuttgart, West Germany and the Museum für Völkerkunde in West Berlin.

Joseph C. Porter, Curator of Western American History and Ethnology, has provided a brief biography of Prince Maximilian entitled *Maximilian, Prince of Wied: A Biographical Sketch,* for this catalogue. The essay entitled *Travels in the Interior of North America,* based on Maximilian's published and unpublished accounts, was compiled by Marsha V. Gallagher, Curator of Material Culture, and David C. Hunt, Curator of Western American Art. Ms. Gallagher and Mr. Hunt also served as curators of this exhibition. John C. Ewers, Ethnologist Emeritus, Smithsonian Institution, has written an illuminating and insightful essay entitled *An Appreciation of Karl Bodmer's Pictures of Indians.*

This exhibition is unique because it brings together the written account as recorded by Maximilian, the visual depiction as executed by Bodmer, and the objects which were described by these two men. The total effect is one of recreating this era, and provides a special opportunity to acquaint the American public with these men, their epic expedition, and their views of America's wilderness frontier.

Henry Flood Robert, Jr.
Director
Joslyn Art Museum

Maximilian, Prince of Wied

A Biographical Sketch

by Joseph C. Porter

1.
Prince Maximilian of Wied with His Brother Prince Charles
Prince Charles zu Wied
Oil on canvas
The InterNorth Art Foundation/
Joslyn Art Museum

This portrait by Prince Charles of himself and his brother was done after Maximilian's return from North America. Maximilian is the shorter of the pair.

2.
Travellers Meeting with Minatarre [Hidatsa] Indians
After Karl Bodmer
Engraving with aquatint; hand-colored
The InterNorth Art Foundation/
Joslyn Art Museum

In 1833 a delegation of Hidatsa dignitaries formally greeted Maximilian's entourage at Fort Clark on the upper Missouri. Karl Bodmer stands at the extreme right of the picture, the Prince beside him in dark coat and hat.

On April 10, 1833, Prince Maximilian of Wied, accompanied by artist Karl Bodmer and personal retainer David Dreidoppel, boarded the American Fur Company steamboat *Yellow Stone* to begin his odyssey up the Missouri River. Maximilian was not the first explorer on the river, but he proved to be one of the most important. Lewis and Clark had taken the Missouri to the Rocky Mountains and had traveled far beyond in 1805-06. In 1832, one year before Maximilian, the American artist George Catlin had reached Fort Union. Yet Maximilian's journey was unique because no explorers other than Lewis and Clark had traveled as far up the untamed Missouri to that time. Likewise, no previous expedition up the river had included both a talented artist-illustrator and an experienced scientist-naturalist.

Maximilian's written accounts and the art of Karl Bodmer caught the upper Missouri River in the midst of profound change. A few years earlier they could not have encountered the Indian peoples who traded at Fort Union or Fort McKenzie. Maximilian witnessed the fur trade, then the primary contact between white and red cultures, flourishing at the trading posts of Fort Pierre, Fort Clark, Fort Union, and Fort McKenzie. Three years later, in 1837, a smallpox epidemic nearly annihilated the Mandans with whom Maximilian wintered in 1833-34. Maximilian and Bodmer saw a transforming western frontier and their observations became the foundation of much of our knowledge and memory of that changing time and place.

Demonstrating his strength of character and personal interests, Maximilian's work was also a part of the intellectual currents within European culture dating from the Spanish discovery of the New World. After 1500, generations of geographers, naturalists, self-styled ethnologists, and intellectuals sought to explore and map newly discovered oceans and continents, to study and classify the multitude of plants and animals, and to ponder the variety of human cultures throughout the world. Exploration fired interest in geography, natural history, and ethnology. The intellectual ferment created by the Age of Discovery revitalized European thought and galvanized the energies of Europe's most adventuresome spirits.

By breeding or background, Maximilian perhaps does not seem the type to have spent his life exploring the wildernesses of distant lands. Nevertheless, aside from his military service in the Napoleonic Wars, he devoted a large part of his energy to the study of natural history and ethnology. The eighth of ten children of the ruling Prince of Wied, Maximilian was born in 1782. As a boy he became interested in natural history.

Later as a student at the University of Göttingen, Maximilian came under the influence of Professor Johann Friedrich Blumenbach. A physiologist, comparative anatomist, and the reputed father of the discipline of physical anthropology, Blumenbach had examined the different races and varieties of mankind around the world. By 1795, five years before Maximilian first studied at the University of Göttingen, Blumenbach possessed one of the finest collections of anthropologia in Europe consisting of eighty-two human skulls, samples of human hair, and "first-hand portraits of representatives of the different human varieties."

3.
Scene on the 'Janus'
Karl Bodmer
Watercolor on paper
The InterNorth Art Foundation/
Joslyn Art Museum

The central seated figure is Maximilian, recording his observations as he did virtually every day for the two years of the journey.

Blumenbach's analysis of cranial comparisons convinced him that all human beings belonged to a single species divided into five races which he labeled as Mongolian, American, Caucasian, Malay, and Ethiopian. Blumenbach also was concerned with the climate and natural habitat where different human groups lived, and he stressed close scientific observation of facts, and the collecting of specimens.

Blumenbach was the direct inspiration for several explorers, including Maximilian. In 1815 the Prince began a two-year expedition in Brazil where his work reflected the influence of Blumenbach and other naturalists of the European Enlightenment. He examined the Brazilian flora, fauna, environment, Indians, especially the Camacans and the Botocudos, and he amassed collections of material. He even purchased two slaves, a Botocudo native and a black, both of whom he took back to Germany.

In his zeal to acquire specimens and record factual details, Maximilian serves as a good example of the early nineteenth century naturalist at work. Observation, description, and classification were the goals of these naturalists. Details and discrete facts formed the bedrock of their study, which compelled them to avidly collect plant, animal, and even human specimens from all around the globe. True to his science, Maximilian used his specimens and observations as the core of his later writing about Brazil, and he followed a similar pattern of collection, observation, and eventual publication for his North American studies.

North America's relatively unexplored wilderness areas and their intriguing variety of flora, fauna, and Indian cultures had long appealed to Maximilian. As early as 1811, four years before going to Brazil, he expressed a desire to visit North America. While he was writing about Brazil he planned his expedition to North America. Methodical and disciplined, he prepared carefully for his next venture,

4.
View of Bethlehem on the Lehigh
Karl Bodmer
Watercolor on paper
The InterNorth Art Foundation/
Joslyn Art Museum

5.
**View of Coal Mine near Mauch
Chunk, with Railroad**
Karl Bodmer
Watercolor on paper
The InterNorth Art Foundation/
Joslyn Art Museum

The small mining town of Mauch
Chunk was one of the places Maximilian visited during his stay at
Bethlehem, Pennsylvania in the
summer of 1832.

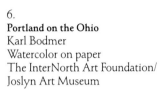

6.
Portland on the Ohio
Karl Bodmer
Watercolor on paper
The InterNorth Art Foundation/
Joslyn Art Museum

reading everything that he could find about North America, especially the works
of other explorers and naturalists. He studied the volumes resulting from the Lewis
and Clark expedition and Major Stephen H. Long's exploration of the Great Plains.
He examined the books of Thomas Nuttall, Duke Paul of Württemberg, and Henry
Marie Brackenridge, among others.

When Maximilian left Europe for the United States in the spring of 1832 he was
better informed about the American wilderness than were most Americans. He
continued his education after his arrival in the United States. In Philadelphia he
visited the Peale Museum to inspect its natural history and ethnographic collections.
The Lewis and Clark and Long expeditions had furnished many of the items
exhibited at the Peale Museum. Its proprietor, Titian Peale, who had served as a
naturalist with Major Long, favorably impressed Maximilian. At the Peale Museum
he also looked at works by Samuel Seymour, another artist with the Long expedition, and saw examples of Charles Bird King's Indian portraits which were later
published in Thomas L. McKenney and James Hall's *History of the Indian Tribes of
North America* (3 Vols., Philadelphia, 1836-44).

Maximilian spent his first American winter at New Harmony, Indiana. An
intellectual center having connections with the Academy of Natural Sciences in
Philadelphia, New Harmony boasted an excellent natural history library and was
the home of two veteran naturalists and explorers, Charles-Alexandre Lesueur
and Thomas Say. Lesueur had been around the globe and Say had accompanied
Long on two different frontier expeditions. Maximilian, Say, and Lesueur spent
the winter of 1832-33 collecting zoological specimens and in learned conversation
about American natural history. Karl Bodmer, meanwhile, spent his first summer

7.
View of New Harmony
Karl Bodmer
Watercolor on paper
The InterNorth Art Foundation/
Joslyn Art Museum

and winter in the United States sketching and painting scenes of the eastern seaboard states and along the Ohio for the Prince. His work ranged from natural history studies to landscapes.

At St. Louis in the spring of 1833, Maximilian talked with trappers and traders who had been farther west. One of America's greatest explorers, General William Clark, befriended Maximilian. Clark had been the partner of Meriwether Lewis during their famous expedition of 1804-06. The General permitted the Prince to attend a council where Sauk and Fox Indians argued for the release of their imprisoned leader Black Hawk. Very interested in Indians, Clark had amassed a fine collection of ethnographic items which he showed to Maximilian. Maximilian also met Major Benjamin O'Fallon, Clark's nephew. An important frontier figure, O'Fallon, an Indian agent and trader, allowed Maximilian and Bodmer to view Indian portraits by George Catlin which were stored at O'Fallon's residence. Clark and O'Fallon advised Maximilian to journey up the Missouri River and put him in contact with Pierre Chouteau, Jr. and Kenneth McKenzie, keymen of the American Fur Company.

One instance aptly demonstrates the type of important assistance that Clark and O'Fallon rendered to Maximilian. William Clark had been the cartographer with the Lewis and Clark expedition years before. In 1833 O'Fallon furnished Maximilian with copies of Clark's maps of the Missouri and Yellowstone Rivers. These consisted of thirty-nine sheets, thirty-four of which were tracings from Clark's originals. O'Fallon personally copied the first two sheets himself for Maximilian.

Only twelve years apart in age, General Clark and Prince Maximilian symbolized two generations of western explorers. A talented, largely self-taught man who typified the American enlightenment of the confident, young republic of President

Thomas Jefferson, Clark heartily encouraged Maximilian. A true product of the rough and tumble American frontier, he may have seen in this German aristocrat an explorer persistent enough to follow his own steps up the Missouri.

Maximilian and his party began their journey up the Missouri in April 1833. Thirteen months were to elapse before they returned to St. Louis. Traveling upriver as far as Fort McKenzie above the Marias River in present-day Montana, they returned downriver to Fort Clark where they wintered among the Mandan and Hidatsa Indians. Maximilian recorded his observations and collected animal specimens while Bodmer sketched and painted. Both witnessed and depicted many aspects of Plains Indian life. The winter at Fort Clark permitted Maximilian the time to conduct his most significant fieldwork among the Mandan and Hidatsa as he studied their languages, cultures, and histories.

Even as Maximilian retraced his route through the eastern United States, he continued to seek out fellow travelers and explorers. In Albany, New York he met Dr. Edwin James, chronicler of Major Long's expedition of 1819-20. In Philadelphia he returned to the Peale Museum and sought out Peter DuPonceneau, a pioneer scholar of American Indian languages. Even in the waning days of his North American journey, Maximilian still sought information about the continent's wildlife and native cultures. He returned to Europe in August 1834, having spent more than two years in North America.

For the rest of his life, Maximilian maintained his interest in North America. He continued to read, study, and write extensively about it. In addition to his two-volume published account of his travels, *Reise in das Innere Nord-America in den Jahren 1832 bis 1834,* he also later published at least twenty articles devoted to North American wildlife in German scientific journals.

The extent of his Brazilian and North American collections and related publications testify that Maximilian was a diligent scholar, but they tell little about the man himself. Very little of his personality is directly revealed in his journals or his published writings, yet an intriguing and complex man emerges from a careful reading between the lines. The business-like tone of his writing hides a person who was capable of earning the friendship and winning the confidence of a wide range of individuals from a variety of backgrounds. His expedition should not be regarded as simply a white encounter with red culture, but rather as a meeting of many cultures, red and white.

Before reaching the Indians, Maximilian had already demonstrated that he could breach the cultural barriers that existed between a learned German nobleman and the turbulent frontier personalities of Jacksonian America. He established genuine friendships with such varied people as Scottish aristocrat William Drummond Stewart, explorer-artist Titian Peale, naturalist Thomas Say, explorer William Clark, and hard-bitten frontier entrepreneurs like Kenneth McKenzie and Pierre Chouteau, Jr. On the Missouri River journey he won the comradeship of trading post managers like James Kipp, David Mitchell, and the dandyish but tough James Hamilton. The key link between the American Fur Company and the various Indian tribes of the Upper Missouri, these men often married women of prominent Indian families and they became Maximilian's entrée to their wives' people.

8.
Confluence of the Fox River and the Wabash
Karl Bodmer
Watercolor on paper
The InterNorth Art Foundation/
Joslyn Art Museum

9.
The Steamboat 'Yellow Stone'
Karl Bodmer
Watercolor on paper
The InterNorth Art Foundation/
Joslyn Art Museum

Prince Maximilian early gained the confidence of veteran frontier hunters and residents like Dechamp, Jacob Berger, and the ancient Toussaint Charbonneau. The Prince possessed the force of character combined with the empathetic nature so essential to any student of cultures. It was critical to his fieldwork that he was capable of earning the trust of individuals like Mató-Tópe, Dipäuch, and Addíh-Hiddísch, all "worthy men" who became important sources of information about their respective peoples, the Mandan and the Hidatsa. They worried about Maximilian's welfare and frequently invited him to attend their ceremonies, dances and feasts. Occasionally they exchanged gifts with him.

The relationship between Maximilian and many of the Indians transcended that of scholar and informant and ripened into friendship. Some Mandans like Mató-Tópe, Síh-Chidä and Dipäuch, or Hidatsas like Péhriska-Rúhpa and Addíh-Hiddísch actively furthered Maximilian's research into the life of their people. Addíh-Hiddísch, a chief at Awaxawi village, willingly shared the history of his tribe, and a prominent Mandan, Dipäuch, contributed greatly to Maximilian's study of Mandan religious beliefs and material culture.

A cooperative effort between Dipäuch and Karl Bodmer resulted in Bodmer's detailed depiction of the interior of a Mandan earth lodge. While the rest of the Mandan moved from their summer lodges to winter dwellings in December of 1833, Dipäuch and his family remained behind for several days so that Bodmer could complete his study of the earth lodge. When Maximilian left Fort Clark in April 1834, he said farewell to many friends among the Mandan and Hidatsa.

Remaining active for the rest of his long life, Maximilian studied, wrote and continued to add to his faunal collections. He hoped to explore the Baltic Sea area and southern Russia, but his advancing age prevented him from doing so. To the last he kept abreast of new developments in the field of natural history, including the work of Charles Darwin, whose ideas and theories forever altered the intellectual landscape so familiar to the naturalists of Maximilian's era.

Prince Maximilian of Wied died in 1867 at the age of eighty-four. He compiled tremendous collections of Americana comprised of material ranging from ethnographic to zoological, botanical, physiological, artistic and historic. Even before he reached St. Louis in the spring of 1833 he had already filled and shipped to Germany nineteen cases of collection material. During the summer and autumn of that year he accumulated another twelve cases which he likewise dispatched. But the artworks of Karl Bodmer and Maximilian's written and published records remain the essential part of the legacy of the Maximilian-Bodmer expedition.

Although Maximilian and Bodmer are now long dead, their adventures on the Missouri frontier live again in *Views of a Vanishing Frontier.* One hundred and fifty years have passed since they explored North America, and much has dramatically changed in the interim. As the future brings more change, their written and painted portraits of our past will become increasingly important.

10.
Bellevue Agency, Post of Major Dougherty
Karl Bodmer
Watercolor on paper
The InterNorth Art Foundation/
Joslyn Art Museum

Travels in the Interior of North America

An Account Drawn from the Published and Unpublished Manuscripts of Prince Maximilian of Wied

*by Marsha V. Gallagher
and David C. Hunt*

11.
**Wahktägeli (Gallant Warrior),
Yankton Sioux Chief**
Karl Bodmer
Watercolor on paper
The InterNorth Art Foundation/
Joslyn Art Museum

Wahktägeli was almost six and
one-half feet tall and was called
"Big Soldier" by the Americans.
The feathers worn on his head
were symbols of his war deeds, and
the human hair fringing his shirt
had been taken by him from
enemies in battle.

12.
Leggings
Upper Missouri
Hide, quills, paint, beads, hair
(human and horse)
The University Museum,
University of Pennsylvania

Plains dress leggings were often
adorned with bands of beadwork
or porcupine quill embroidery and
with long fringes of leather or hair.
They were also frequently painted.
The colors and stripes or other
patterns were not simply decorative but could also represent
numbers or types of exploits, such
as enemies touched or killed in
battle. The leggings pictured here
may have originally been collected
by artist George Catlin, who
visited Upper Missouri posts in
1832.

aximilian's voyage to North America began on the morning of May 7, 1832 when he departed the family estate at Neuwied for the Dutch port of Rotterdam on the Rhine steamer *Concordia*. With him were Swiss artist Karl Bodmer, under contract to produce a visual documentary of the Prince's intended travels, and David Dreidoppel, Maximilian's personal servant and an experienced hunter and taxidermist. The Prince's diary entries on even those first days of travel reflect his wide interests and careful observation of his surroundings. In Rotterdam he remarked on the weather ("adverse winds"), the ships in the harbor ("2 frigates and 3 war-brigs, 5 gunboats, each with one mast, 2 yards and a short bowsprit and 5 cannons. . . ."), and the types of birds nesting in the trees there.

On the evening of May 17 the travelers boarded an American brig, *Janus*, bound for Boston. Passage down the English Channel and around Great Britain's southern coast required a week of sailing; on the 24th they "saw Land's End, Cornwall, vanish in the misty distance, and bade farewell to Europe." The *Janus* encountered heavy seas during the first two weeks of June. The voyage was otherwise relatively uneventful, although the three men, particularly young Bodmer, suffered bouts of seasickness.

Cape Cod was sighted on July 3 and on the following morning the *Janus* entered the port of Boston to the sound of cannons fired in celebration of the fifty-sixth anniversary of the United States' independence from Great Britain. From the moment of their arrival in North America, the travelers from Europe were never idle. Maximilian had planned his itinerary well and carried letters of introduction to several prominent German-American citizens and scholars in the various cities and settlements he intended to visit on his way westward across the United States. In Boston and at other stops he purchased books, maps and supplies for his scientific studies. He visited museums, finding them generally disappointing, and made excursions to local points of interest, such as the recently begun monument at Bunker's Hill. The city inhabitants were, he thought, elegantly and perhaps overly dressed. The "large and much frequented inns of the great towns in the United States are in many respects inferior to those of Europe" and the table manners of the guests left something to be desired: " . . . they rush tumultuously into the eating-room. . . . Then everyone takes possession of the dish he can first lay his hands on, and in ten minutes all is consumed; in laconic silence the company rise from table, put on their hats, and . . . hasten away. . . ."

The travelers proceeded to Providence and then to New York, despite reports of cholera there, a factor which altered Maximilian's original itinerary. " . . . This lamentable disease had been very fatal in Canada and had now penetrated into the Northern States of the Union; it was raging in Albany, on the Hudson, at Detroit, and on the Great Lakes, so that it seemed as if it would defeat our project of beginning our journey to the interior by that route." On July 16, Maximilian went on alone to Philadelphia, leaving Bodmer and Dreidoppel to wait impatiently for the delivery of their baggage, which was still delayed at Boston.

In Philadelphia Maximilian explored the countryside as well as the "splendid" shops and principal public buildings of the city. He used his letters of introduction to meet German residents, but missed making the acquaintance of "several scientific

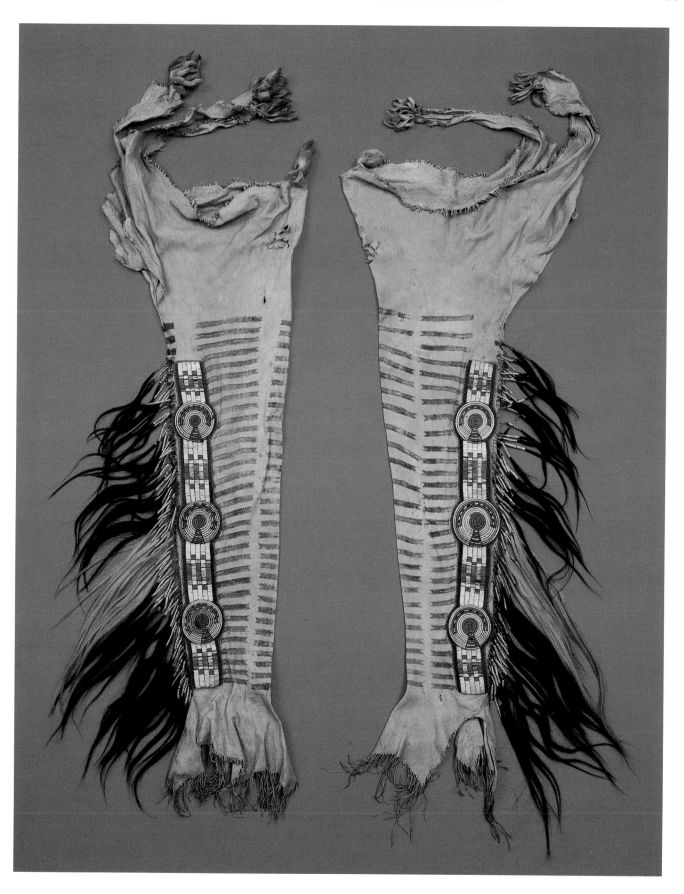

13.

Assiniboin Medicine Sign
Karl Bodmer
Watercolor on paper
The InterNorth Art Foundation/
Joslyn Art Museum

This shrine-like arrangement of a
buffalo skull on a rock was one of
many Maximilian saw in the area
around Fort Union. He called them
"medicine signs," magical devices
placed by the Assiniboin to lure the
buffalo herds on which the people
depended for existence.

14.
Assiniboin Camp
Karl Bodmer
Watercolor on paper
The InterNorth Art Foundation/
Joslyn Art Museum

gentleman, because, being physicians, they were now particularly engaged" with treating cholera, which had spread to Philadelphia. He did, however, see Titian Peale, the artist-naturalist who had accompanied the Plains expedition of Major Stephen Long in 1819-20, and eagerly examined the specimens from the expedition at the museum operated by the Peale family. The Prince praised this museum "for its more scientific arrangement, and because fewer trifling nicknacks have been allowed into it." The paintings of Indians by Samuel Seymour, another artist on the Long expedition, particularly interested Maximilian, who was astonished that he could not find any good, published illustrations of America's aboriginal peoples. "It is incredible how much the original American race is hated and neglected by the foreign usurpers."

Bodmer and Dreidoppel finally arrived, but without the baggage. Nonetheless, the party headed north to Bethlehem on July 30. The month of August was spent in the vicinity of this predominantly German town, at that time a settlement of about a thousand persons. On the evening of his arrival in Bethlehem, Maximilian met a German physician and naturalist, Lewis David von Saynisch, who subsequently accompanied him on several outings as Maximilian began in earnest to collect native flora and fauna. By September he had accumulated five crates of specimens to ship back to Europe: 170 birds, 43 turtles, 40-50 snakes and about 40 frogs and toads. Bodmer occasionally assisted in making these collections but occupied himself primarily with sketching local points of interest.

Maximilian and Dreidoppel, leaving Bodmer temporarily behind, left Bethlehem on September 17. They took the Easton stage for Harrisburg where they spent two days while Maximilian sought the advice of a local physician for what he termed "an exhausted, ailing state of health." Bodmer rejoined the party before they reached Pittsburgh. From there Maximilian made a side trip to "the remarkable and interesting colony" of Economy, the third of three utopian settlements established by George Rapp. Maximilian was impressed by Rapp and his self-sufficient commune, particularly with the extensive fields and vineyards and "several important manufactories with steam engines." The arrangement and direction "of this artificial society are admirable and do honour to the founder."

A few days later the three men went to Wheeling on the Ohio River, where they boarded the *Nile,* "a small vessel, because steamers of a large size cannot come so high up the river." They changed ships at Cincinnati and again at Portland, below Louisville. The specter of cholera continued to haunt them. At Cincinnati forty people a day were dying of the disease, and five days later a passenger on the steamboat "declared himself ill early in the morning and was dead before eleven o'clock." On October 18, when the travelers disembarked at Mount Vernon, Indiana, and made arrangements to go by wagon to New Harmony fifteen miles away, Maximilian was again feeling unwell. His stay at New Harmony, "at first intended to be only for a few days, was prolonged by serious indisposition, nearly resembling cholera, to a four months' winter residence."

New Harmony had been founded by Rapp in 1814, but in 1825 the theocratic

15.
Shield Cover
Upper Missouri
Hide, paint
National Museum of Natural History, Smithsonian Institution
Photo courtesy of National Anthropological Archives, Smithsonian Institution

The bear was a symbol of strong supernatural power. The unknown warrior who painted this early nineteenth century shield cover, from the War Department collection, evidently sought after that power as a protective device. As John C. Ewers has speculated, the black dashes appear to depict enemy gunfire warded off by the strength of the grizzly bear, represented by the large red paw in the center of the cover ("The Awesome Bear in Plains Indian Art," *American Indian Art,* Summer 1982, p. 42).

16.
Noapéh (Troop of Soldiers),
Assiniboin Man
Karl Bodmer
Watercolor on paper
The InterNorth Art Foundation/
Joslyn Art Museum

The antelope horn headdress worn
by Noapéh was described by
Maximilian as being trimmed with
black feathers and yellow horsehair
and quillwork. Maximilian wished
to buy it but Noapéh would not
part with it. His refusal to sell suggests that the headdress had strong
ceremonial significance or was a
personal "medicine", perhaps an
association with the swiftness of
the antelope.

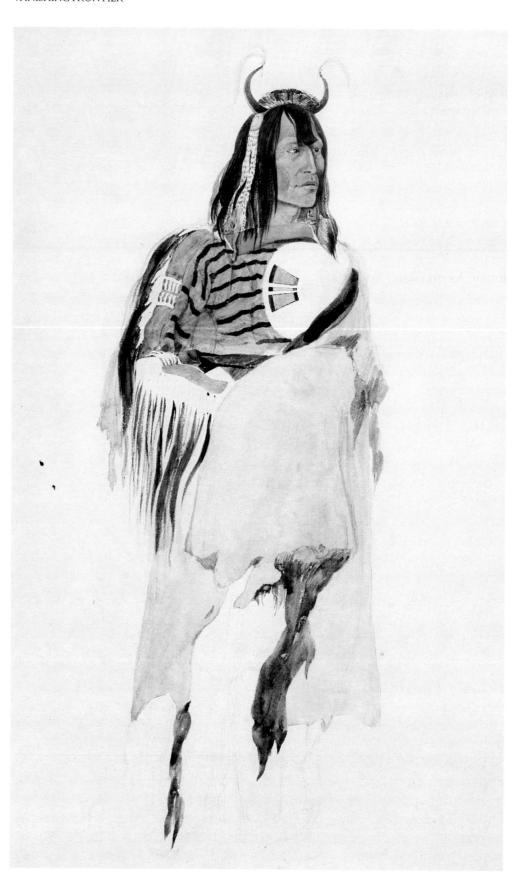

commune sold its land and buildings to Robert Owen and moved to Economy, the settlement Maximilian had visited near Pittsburgh. Owen, a prominent English social reformer, and William Maclure, the president of Philadelphia's Academy of Natural Sciences, sought to establish at New Harmony a different sort of utopian society based on education. Maclure brought several scientists to New Harmony with the idea of starting an agricultural school, among them two eminent naturalists, Thomas Say and Charles-Alexandre Lesueur. It was these men Maximilian came to see.

Say, an entomologist, had been on two frontier explorations with Major Long. Lesueur was a skilled artist, highly respected for his scientific studies in Australia as well as North America. Maximilian was delighted at the opportunity to be instructed by these two experienced scholars, and to make use of their extensive natural history library. As his health improved the Prince avidly explored the forests around New Harmony, adding specimens to his constantly growing botanical and zoological collection and filling his journal with observations on the flora and fauna. With Lesueur he examined archaeological sites: "Like the whole of the interior of North America, the country on the Wabash has still numerous traces of a very early extinct original population...and the present white population may justly be reproached for neglecting or destroying...these remarkable remains of antiquity." Maximilian also had much to say concerning the settlers and living conditions on the frontier. New Harmony was "a relatively advanced cultural community...composed mostly of farmers...and owners of plantations." The fertile land around it had attracted large numbers of pioneers, "a robust, rough race of men."

On the whole, however, Maximilian was not favorably impressed with the frontier settlements of Indiana and Illinois, commenting that "by way of settlement, we may preserve here in America neither the aborigines nor the wild beasts, because the beginning of settlement is always the destruction of everything...." He estimated that within a few years deer, wolves, and wild turkeys would no longer be seen in the area, remarking that "the elks, bears, and beavers have already vanished, and the rest will follow soon."

During the months of November and December, Bodmer went frequently to the banks of the Fox and Wabash Rivers. His representations of the forested banks of these streams reveal the young artist's love of nature and show a freedom of expression not as easily realized within the formal constraints of scientific illustration and portraiture.

In January 1833 Bodmer went alone by steamboat to New Orleans, where he stayed with a friend of Lesueur's. When he returned a month later he gave Maximilian a full account of all he had seen, including groups of Cherokee and Choctaw. This report undoubtedly increased Maximilian's impatience to continue his journey and to see for himself the "many tribes of the aborigines." In March Maximilian prepared to depart New Harmony for St. Louis, and the party embarked on an Ohio steamer at Mount Vernon on the morning of the 18th. The ensuing voyage

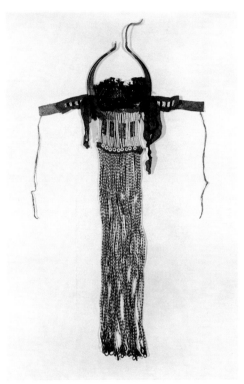

17.
Headdress
Upper Missouri, Assiniboin style
Antelope horn, hide, cloth, feathers, quills, beads, horsehair
Courtesy of the Museum of the American Indian, Heye Foundation

This headdress, although undocumented as to date or original source, is likely mid-nineteenth century. It is markedly similar to the one shown in Plate 16.

18.
**Junction of the Yellowstone and
the Missouri**
Karl Bodmer
Watercolor on paper
The InterNorth Art Foundation/
Joslyn Art Museum

downriver was quickly accomplished, and the *Paragon* passed from the Ohio to the Mississippi River on March 20. Four days later the travelers landed at St. Louis and made their way to the Union Hotel where Maximilian found waiting for him a letter from Germany dated November 21 of the previous year.

From March 24 through April 10, 1833, Maximilian's journal describes his stay at St. Louis, then the gateway to the trans-Mississippi West and a rowdy, rapidly growing frontier trading center. Here he met several individuals who were to prove helpful to his plans for wilderness travel, including former explorer William Clark, then serving as superintendent of Indian affairs for the western tribes. General Clark gave Maximilian copies of maps of the Upper Missouri region first surveyed on his expedition with Meriwether Lewis in 1804-06. These hand-drawn sheets recorded the river route from present-day Omaha, Nebraska to Great Falls, Montana.

Maximilian also met Kenneth McKenzie and Pierre Chouteau, Jr. of the American Fur Company, men thoroughly familiar with the northern plains. At the house of Major Benjamin O'Fallon, Clark's nephew, he inspected a collection of Indian portraits by George Catlin, who only the year before had visited the fur company posts on the upper Missouri and had painted the natives of that region.

From the city's resident artist, Peter Rindisbacher, he ordered several watercolors of Indian subjects. Bodmer meanwhile made studies of several Sauk and Fox Indians who were part of a delegation in St. Louis to plead for the release of Black Hawk, a chief who had been imprisoned after the hostilities of 1832. Maximilian was permitted to observe a council between General Clark and these tribal represent-

19.
Beaver Lodge on the Missouri
Karl Bodmer
Watercolor on paper
The InterNorth Art Foundation/
Joslyn Art Museum

On July 17, 1833, above Fort
Union, Maximilian noted a beaver
den. He commented on the general
construction of such dens and their
spacious interior chambers, and
expressed regret that there was not
enough time to enter and personally inspect this one.

atives, which was, as he said, his first opportunity to personally "observe and study
these remarkable people."

In choosing his route into the western interior, Maximilian first considered going
overland to the Rocky Mountains and the Spanish colonial capital of Santa Fe.
Captain William Drummond Stewart, a Scotch adventurer, "was on the point of
setting out . . . by caravan, and it would have been agreeable for me to travel in his
company." But experienced frontiersmen like Clark advised Maximilian instead
to travel up the Missouri River under the protection of John Jacob Astor's powerful
American Fur Company.

"The Company," as it was called, dominated not only the lucrative Missouri
fur trade, but the administration of Indian affairs as well. At the Company's river
trading posts, contacts with Indians would be more frequent and more friendly
than on the dangerous overland route, subject to hostile attack. Equally important,
the Company's boats could accommodate Maximilian's bulky supplies and
collections more easily than wagons. These vessels were used primarily for transport
of the Company's goods and employees and normally did not take paying pas-
sengers to the upper reaches of the Missouri. But Clark's influence, Maximilian's
family friendship with the Astors, and Chouteau's interest in the scientific project
worked in Maximilian's favor and the necessary arrangements were readily made.

Maximilian purchased some supplies for the voyage in St. Louis. These included
such provisions as "coffee, sugar, brandy, candles, fine gunpowder, shot of every
kind, colours, paper," and numerous articles to trade with the Indians: "calico,

knives, brass bells, burning glasses, cinnabar, red ribbon . . . ." He also deposited $2,000.00 with the Company and took with him a letter of credit against which he could purchase additional supplies at the trading posts.

"On the 10th of April, at eleven o'clock, all our company having collected, the *Yellow Stone* left St. Louis . . . . There were about 100 persons on board . . . , most of whom were those called *engagés* or *voyageurs,* who are the lowest class of [employees] of the Fur Company. Most of them are French Canadians, or descendants of the French settlers on the Mississippi and Missouri."

The *Yellow Stone,* on its maiden voyage in 1832, had been the first steam-powered craft to ascend the Missouri above Council Bluffs in an experiment by the Company to see if steamboats could be substituted for the smaller sail and man-powered keelboats in the trade on the upper river. That trade was booming. In the 1830s the American Fur Company obtained annually from the Upper Missouri tribes as many as 40,000 buffalo hides and 100,000 pelts or skins of other animals: beaver, weasel, lynx, fox, mink, muskrat and deer. In return the Indians received a profusion of merchandise ranging from trinkets, kettles and cloth to guns and liquor.

Travel by steamer on the Missouri was a difficult and dangerous business in 1833. Large boats like the *Yellow Stone,* laden with cargo and Company employees, frequently ran aground on treacherous sandbanks. At many stretches along the river boats had to be poled over shallows or dragged off sandbanks by crews using long ropes or hawsers called *cordelles.* Sometimes cargo had to be unloaded temporarily to lighten the vessel's draft. Storms, contrary currents and sunken trees or snags presented other perils. Difficult to see and avoid, snags often broke the paddles of the wheels or penetrated the ship's side. On April 23 Maximilian reported that "a large branch of a tree, lying in the water, forced its way into the cabin . . . carried away part of the door, and was left on the floor . . . . One might have been crushed in bed . . . ."

The passage from St. Louis to the area of present-day Omaha took about three weeks. There were frequent stops to take on firewood, send hunters ashore to search for game, and to conduct business at posts along the way. Maximilian took advantage of these opportunities to leave the ship in search of specimens, assiduously recording the plant and animal life: "The underwood of the forest consisted chiefly of *Laurus benzoin* and *Cercis Canadensis*; the ground was covered with *Equisetum hymenale,* from one and a half to two feet high." On another day " . . . I was returning to the [ship] when the pilot called out that there was a rattlesnake very near me . . . I looked . . . [and] stunned it with some slight blows [and] put it into a vessel in which there were already a live heterodon and a black snake, where it soon recovered. The three agreed very well together, but were afterwards put into a cask of brandy" to be preserved and sent to Europe.

The *Yellow Stone* was now well into the official "territory of the free Indians." On May 3 the steamer paused briefly at Bellevue, the site of the government agency that administered dealings with the Omaha and other tribes of that region. The next day, at a Company post a few miles upriver, Bodmer sketched two of the many Omaha people who had come there to trade. That evening, at the request of the post's proprietor, Jean Pierre Cabanné, the Omaha performed a ceremonial dance for the travelers, a vivid, moonlit scene that greatly impressed Maximilian.

20.
The White Castles on the Missouri
Karl Bodmer
Watercolor on paper
The InterNorth Art Foundation/
Joslyn Art Museum

Indications of the presence of Indians became more frequent. A small group of Ponca was picked up by the steamer and carried upstream to their camp on May 12. Sioux burial scaffolds were noted near the banks of the river and on May 25, the *Yellow Stone* stopped at Fort Lookout, the Sioux agency. "… The Sioux … are still one of the most numerous Indian tribes in North America …; 20,000 is … not too high an estimate…. [They] are divided into several branches … three [of which] live on the Missouri, viz., the Yanktons …, the Tetons …, and the Yanktonans."

About ten tipis were camped near Fort Lookout and Maximilian visited that of Wahktägeli, a Yankton chief, "a tall, good-looking man … sixty years of age…. On his head he wore feathers of birds of prey, which were [symbols] of his warlike exploits … and … suspended from his neck, the great silver [peace] medal of the United States." Maximilian met many more Yankton and Teton Sioux at Fort Pierre, one of the American Fur Company's largest posts, and his journal is full of descriptive information about the physical appearance, dress and customs of these people. The Prince learned much about the various Plains tribes from the seasoned traders who lived near or with them. The post managers also acted as or provided interpreters for Maximilian so that he could converse with chiefs, warriors and elders.

Maximilian's party spent a week at Fort Pierre. During this time 7,000 buffalo hides and other furs were loaded on to the *Yellow Stone*, which then returned to St. Louis. The voyage upriver was continued on another steamer, the *Assiniboine,* which departed on the 5th of June. At Fort Clark on the 18th the *Assiniboine* was greeted by a deputation of Mandan and Hidatsa leaders, including several men whom Maximilian would come to know later very well when he returned to spend the

21.
**Unusual Formations on the Upper
Missouri**
Karl Bodmer
Watercolor on paper
The InterNorth Art Foundation/
Joslyn Art Museum

22.
Citadel Rock
Karl Bodmer
Watercolor on paper
The InterNorth Art Foundation/
Joslyn Art Museum

Called *La Citadelle* or Citadel Rock
by the traders, this is still one of the
most prominent and readily recognized landmarks on the Missouri
and is today a Montana state
monument.

23.
View of the Stone Walls
Karl Bodmer
Watercolor on paper
The InterNorth Art Foundation/
Joslyn Art Museum

Citadel Rock, Plate 22, was only
one of many breathtaking emi-
nences in the twelve to fifteen mile
stretch of the Missouri known as
the Stone Walls. This and other
watercolors of the area can be com-
pared to the present, little changed
landscape, clear evidence of
Bodmer's accuracy.

winter there. This visit was brief, however, and the *Assiniboine* pushed on to Fort
Union, arriving to the sound of a cannon and musketry salute on June 24. The
voyage from St. Louis, estimated by Maximilian at 2,000 miles, had taken seventy-
five days to complete.

Fort Union was another of the principal posts of the American Fur Company,
located near the junction of the Yellowstone and Missouri Rivers in the territory
of the Assiniboin Indians.

> The fort...forms a quadrangle, the sides of which measure about eighty
> paces in length.... The ramparts consist of strong pickets, sixteen or
> seventeen feet high...surmounted by a *chevaux-de-frise* [a system of
> spikes or barbs]. On the south-west and north-east ends there are block-
> houses...two stories high, with embrasures and some cannon.... In
> the front...is the well-defended [main] entrance, with a large folding
> gate.... In the inner quadrangle are the residences of the [commandant],
> the clerks, the interpreters and the *engagés*, the powder magazine, the
> stores or supplies of goods and bartered skins, various workshops for
> the...smiths, carpenters, etc., stables for the horses and cattle, rooms
> for receiving and entertaining the Indians; and in the centre is the flag-
> staff....

Maximilian also commented on the climate of the area, the natural surroundings of
the fort, the trade conducted there and the Indians who came to trade. "The
Assiniboins are [a branch of the Sioux] which separated from the rest a considerable
time ago...." Like the other nomadic Plains tribes, they subsisted primarily on

the buffalo and were skilled hunters. In cooperative hunts, called surrounds, "the Indians sometimes kill 700 or 800 buffaloes."

Twelve days were spent at Fort Union that summer, a productive time for Bodmer, who sketched the fort, the landscape, the flora, and the Assiniboin. Among the latter subjects were the painted tipi of a chief, a burial scaffold, and several portraits. Assiniboin men visited Maximilian's quarters and smoked with him while these portraits were made; the Prince in turn went to their camps where he observed women at work, a curing ceremony, and other aspects of Assiniboin life.

Fort Union represented the upper limit of steamer traffic on the Missouri in 1833. To go beyond meant travel by keelboat or pack train, and so Maximilian's party boarded the *Flora* on July 6, bound for Fort McKenzie more than 500 miles upriver. The *Flora*, sixty feet long by sixteen broad, had a small cabin in the stern with two berths; Maximilian shared these accommodations with four men. The forty-seven other persons aboard (Company crew, *engagés* destined for employment at Fort McKenzie, and two Indian women) made use of a single forward apartment. Cargo was stored in a central hold, and an iron grate on the deck served as a common kitchen.

Keelboats were fitted with masts and sails, but when there was insufficient wind, going upstream meant backbreaking labor for the crew. Walking along runways on each side of the deck, they struggled to push the keelboat along with poles. Often they had to go ashore with *cordelles* and haul the vessel against the swift current, working their way through thick underbrush and over sometimes perilously high banks and bluffs. Maximilian noted that shifts of sixteen to eighteen men would haul the *Flora* thus for two hours and then try to regain their strength while the next relay strained against the hawsers.

The difficult passage upstream to Fort McKenzie took almost five weeks. This section of the Missouri River is noted for beautiful and sometimes bizarre geological formations, many of which appeared to the travelers as more nearly resembling architecture than nature's art. One series of sculpted bluffs and hills looked like castles "with small perpendicular slits which appeared to be so many windows. These singular natural formations, when seen from a distance, so perfectly resembled buildings . . . that we were deceived by them till we were assured of our error. We agreed . . . to give to these original works of nature the name of 'The White Castles.' "

While Bodmer filled his sketchbook with views of the constantly changing scenery, Maximilian was fully occupied with recording his natural history observations and obtaining specimens. The Prince's enthusiasm was not, however, shared by the crew:

> . . . we had made a numerous and interesting collection of natural history, many articles of which we were obliged, for want of room, to leave on deck. The skins, skulls of animals, and the like, some of which it had cost us much trouble to procure, were generally thrown into the river during the night, though [the Company] had set a penalty of five dollars on such irregularities. In this manner I lost many highly interesting specimens; and on board our keel-boat, with the most favourable oppor-

24.
Piegan Blackfeet Man
Karl Bodmer
Watercolor and pencil on paper
The InterNorth Art Foundation/
Joslyn Art Museum

Plains warriors often painted their
robes or shirts with symbols of
their war deeds. The figures on the
elk hide worn by this Piegan man
indicate that he had many successes
in battle; there are wounded adver-
saries, and many horses, guns and
other weapons stolen from his
enemies.

25.
Shirt
Upper Missouri
Hide, paint, quills, hair
National Museum of Natural
History, Smithsonian Institution
Photo courtesy of National
Anthropological Archives,
Smithsonian Institution

Three war coups are represented on
the back of this shirt, seen here;
two coups are pictured on the front.
Its history is not documented, but
the decorative style suggests that
the garment dates to the early nineteenth century.

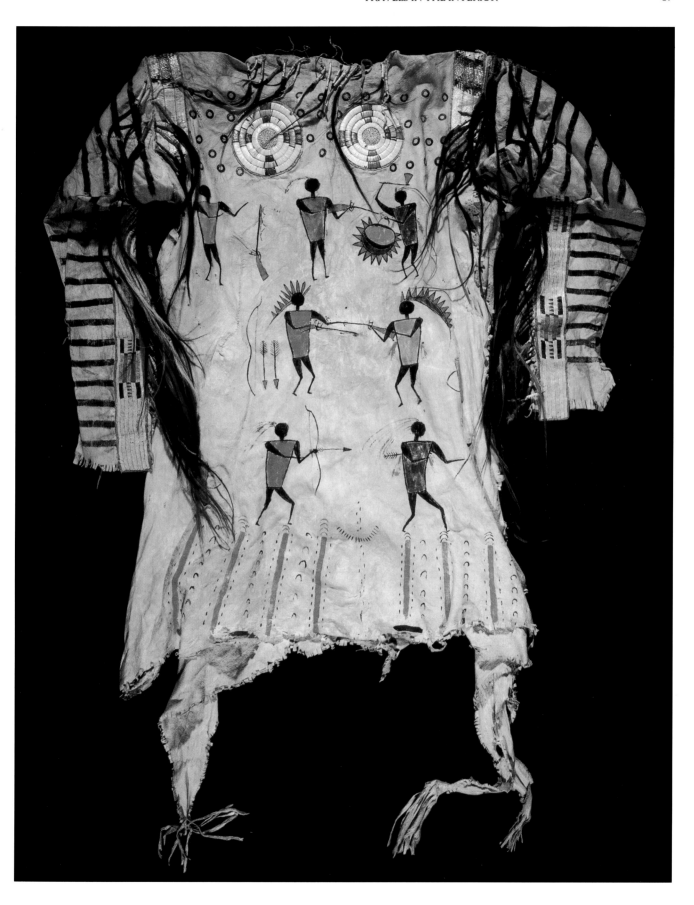

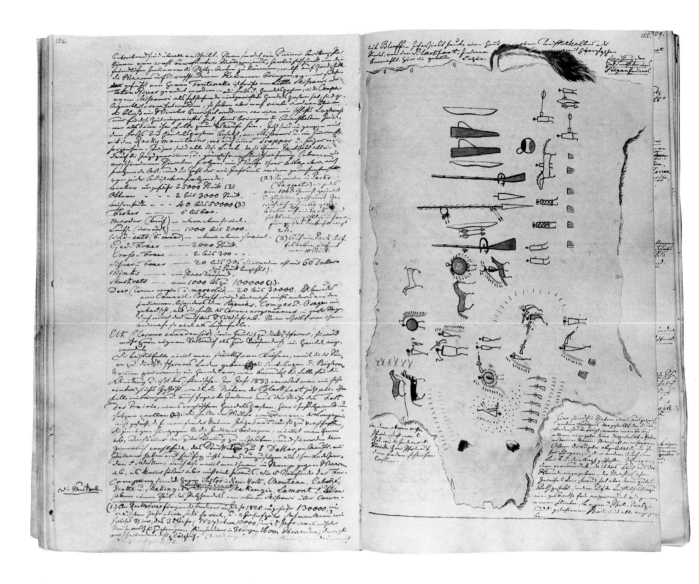

26.
Manuscript Journal, Vol. 2 of 3
Prince Maximilian of Wied
Ink, watercolor on paper (bound)
The InterNorth Art Foundation/
Joslyn Art Museum

Maximilian often sketched
pictures in his journals to illustrate
his written descriptions of objects
or events. Here he has drawn a
painted buffalo hide, which he said
recorded several exploits of one
warrior who was always depicted
in a feathered bonnet. He added
that women were among the vic-
tims of the protagonist, their bodies
drawn as rectangles to differentiate
them from the more pointed figures
of the men.

tunities, it was hardly possible to make a collection of natural history, if
I except the herbarium, which we kept in the cabin, under our eyes, ...
By August 5 the *Flora* was well into the territory of the powerful, warlike Blackfeet.
Few Indians had yet been sighted, but on this date the keelboat came opposite a
large encampment of Atsina, allies of the Blackfeet. Eight chiefs were brought on
board to receive presents. They were quickly followed by swarms of Indians
demanding to trade. " . . . Our keel-boat was suddenly entered on every side . . . . Tall,
slender men covered the deck, thrust themselves into the apartments, and we were
really overwhelmed with them . . . . Our situation was everything but agreeable,
for these same Indians had entirely demolished a fort . . . two years before, killed a
clerk and eighteen other persons . . . . If it was their intention to treat us in a hostile
manner, there was no way to escape." A favorable wind allowed the *Flora* to sail
out of reach; the tension of the moment abated, yet the encounter was a reminder
of the still precarious relationship existing between whites and the warriors of the
northern Plains.

27.
Piegan Blackfeet Woman
Karl Bodmer
Watercolor on paper
The InterNorth Art Foundation/
Joslyn Art Museum

28.
**View of the Highwood Mountains
from Fort McKenzie**
Karl Bodmer
Watercolor on paper
The InterNorth Art Foundation/
Joslyn Art Museum

Four days later the *Flora* arrived at Fort McKenzie, the westernmost outpost of the American Fur Company, established in 1832 as part of the Company's effort to open trade with the hostile Blackfeet. A cautious atmosphere of friendship prevailed at the moment, and the keelboat was greeted by 800 Blackfeet men and throngs of women and children. In the month spent at the fort, Maximilian met many important leaders and, through an interpreter, learned much about tribal tradition and history. "The Blackfeet form a numerous nation, which is divided into three tribes . . . [the Siksika or Northern Blackfeet; the Kainah or Blood; and the Pikuni or Piegan] . . . . As they speak only one language, keep together, and differ but little in their external appearance, they are justly considered as one and the same nation . . . . "

Page after page in Maximilian's journal is devoted to his observations on the Blackfeet: their appearance, clothing and ornament; their tipis and pack animals; food and medicine; marriage customs; men's societies; and behavior in battle. In regard to the latter, Maximilian was an unwilling participant-observer when, on the morning of August 28, almost 600 Assiniboin and Cree mounted a surprise attack on the Blackfeet camped outside the fort. Many Indians were killed or wounded and all was confusion and noise, both within and without the fort, before the enemy was forced to retreat.

29.
Buffalo and Elk on the Upper Missouri
Karl Bodmer
Watercolor on paper
The InterNorth Art Foundation/
Joslyn Art Museum

In going to Fort McKenzie, Maximilian had originally intended to continue overland to the Rocky Mountains. But the Assiniboin attack was clear evidence of the potential danger of such an undertaking. Even the Blackfeet advised him against traveling through their territory. The Piegan chief Tátsicki-Stomíck said that his people would not harm them, but he could not speak for the Siksika or Kainah and, in any event, the horses so necessary for survival would inevitably make them the target of raids. The practical scientist therefore resolved to return downriver: "We had…[become] well acquainted with the Blackfeet Indians, and collected a great number of interesting portraits of them, and could not hope…to add [specimens] to our collection" during the winter months ahead. David Mitchell, the manager of the post, arranged for an oar-powered Mackinaw boat to be constructed, which the Prince lamented as being too small. The cases containing his collections and a large cage with two live bears filled most of the boat, leaving cramped quarters for Maximilian, Bodmer, Dreidoppel, a pilot, and a somewhat inexperienced crew of three.

The voyage began auspiciously enough on September 14, a fine and bright morning, but that night a cold, heavy rain numbed the men, for the open boat offered no shelter. Worse, the rain soaked all their effects and, though the men laboriously unpacked all the chests and crates and spread out the contents to dry,

30.
Evening Bivouac on the Upper Missouri
Karl Bodmer
Watercolor on paper
The InterNorth Art Foundation/
Joslyn Art Museum

This scene, a finished composition, was probably executed in Europe from memory or field sketches. It depicts one of the temporary camps made on the quick return downriver from Fort Union to Fort Clark in November of 1833. The cages for the bears can be seen near the stern of the Mackinaw boat.

much was ruined. "What grieved me most was that all my botanical collection, which I had made . . . with many efforts and perseverance . . . , appeared to be completely lost."

The weather became more favorable and the party progressed rapidly downriver, taking advantage of the strong current. They even traveled by moonlight to hasten the journey, for they felt vulnerable to Indian attack. Fort Union was reached on September 29, the fifteen day return accomplished in less than half the time it had taken to go upstream earlier that summer.

Although he was invited to pass the winter at Fort Union, Maximilian preferred to go on to Fort Clark in order to study the Mandan and Hidatsa. He made arrangements to exchange his small Mackinaw boat for a more commodious one which, however, required extensive repairs and refitting. While this was being done he made further observations on the Assiniboin who came to the fort, and also met some Cree and Ojibwa. Provisions were scarce and Maximilian and Bodmer participated in a buffalo hunt to help restock the larder. The traders relied on game for food as much as did the Indians. About 600 to 800 buffaloes were consumed annually at Fort Union and hunters generally went out twice a week.

31.
Mandan Shrine
Karl Bodmer
Watercolor on paper
The InterNorth Art Foundation/
Joslyn Art Museum

Maximilian saw many shrines
near the Mandan village of Mih-
Tutta-Hang-Kusch. This one was
dedicated to two principal deities,
The Lord of Life and The Old
Woman Who Never Dies. The
man standing before the shrine is
most likely a supplicant seeking the
supernatural help of these sacred
beings.

32.
**Mandeh-Kahchu (Eagle's Beak),
Mandan Man**
Karl Bodmer
Watercolor and pencil on paper
The InterNorth Art Foundation/
Joslyn Art Museum

The Plains Indians' love of ornament is evident in many of
Bodmer's portraits, particularly in
this one of a dandyish young Mandan man. His hair is lavishly
adorned with bands of fur, a heavy
beaded dangle, and hairbows with
long strings of beads and dentalium
shells. The multiple earrings are
probably made of abalone shell, the
large choker necklace fashioned
from rolls of buckskin covered with
beadwork. Mandeh-Kahchu was
the brother of the man pictured in
Plate 34.

The area around Fort Union had changed markedly since July, taking on the colors of autumn. Snow fell on October 15 and the midday temperatures were not much above freezing. Maximilian kept a daily log of morning and noontime temperatures, except when circumstances prevented this; his thermometer was the subject of much curiosity by the Indians and was stolen and recovered more than once.

The boat was finally made ready. On the morning of October 30, Maximilian thanked James Hamilton, who had been his generous host at Fort Union, and cast off for Fort Clark. Ten days later, "...we saw the...Mandan village [of] Mih-Tutta-Hang-Kusch and, at no great distance beyond it, Fort Clark, which we reached at four o'clock, and were welcomed on shore by Mr. Kipp, the director and clerk of the Fur Company, who led us to his house."

Since accommodations at Fort Clark were apparently already crowded, a new building was ordered to house the three visitors. The work had to be done hastily, for winter had definitely arrived. The result was a "slightly built" dwelling that offered little protection from the cold:

> The large crevices in the wood which formed the wall, were plastered up with clay, but the frost soon cracked it, so that the bleak wind penetrated on all sides. Our new house, which was one story high, consisted of two light, spacious apartments, with large glass windows; we inhabited one of these rooms, while the other served for a workshop for the carpenter and the joiner. Each room had a brick [fireplace].... On the 22nd of November we took possession...[although] the whitewashed walls were still damp, and the constant wind filled [the house] with smoke. We were, however, thankful to have space to carry on our labours, to which we now applied with great assiduity, to make up for the time we had lost. The large windows afforded a good light for drawing, and we had a couple of small tables and some benches of poplar wood, and three shelves against the walls, on which we spread our blankets and buffaloes' skins, and reposed during the night. The room was floored; the door was furnished with bolts on the inside, and the fire-wood, covered with frozen snow, was piled up close to the chimney.

The weather became increasingly bitter; by mid-December the noon thermometer readings were never above freezing. "On the 3rd [of January, 1834] the mercury sank into the ball and was frozen; it remained there on the 4th, but on the 5th it rose, and at eight in the morning was 9° below zero [Fahrenheit].... At night the cold was so intense, that we could not venture to put our hands from our bodies, lest they should be frozen.... [Our] boots and shoes were frozen so hard in the morning, that we could scarcely put them on; ink, colours, and pencils were perfectly useless" till they were thawed by the fire.

The frigid weather was not the only hardship, for food was in short supply. Game, which normally formed a major part of the diet, was hard to find. A list kept by Maximilian suggests that the Fort Clark hunters shot less than a dozen

33.
Choker Necklace
Upper Missouri
Hide, beads, metal
National Museum of Natural
History, Smithsonian Institution
Photo courtesy of National
Anthropological Archives,
Smithsonian Institution

Originally collected from the Sioux
in 1855, this necklace may be many
years older. The style was pictured
by both Bodmer (see Plate 32) and
by George Catlin.

buffaloes and very little else that entire winter, and the fort inhabitants were often without meat. On December 26 "we had now no meat [and] our breakfast consisted of coffee and maize bread, and our dinner of maize bread and bean soup." Supplies dwindled and by March "our diet consisted almost exclusively of maize boiled in water, which greatly weakened our digestion."

But for Maximilian the privations were more than offset by the opportunity to study and describe in detail the Mandan, "a small tribe which has hitherto been very imperfectly known," and their close geographic and cultural neighbors, the Hidatsa. He was invited to a ceremony shortly after his arrival, the first of many he attended in the ensuing months. He observed people at work and at play and received a steady stream of visitors, among them many eminent chiefs and learned elders. Intent on obtaining "exact information," Maximilian queried his guests on subjects ranging from agricultural practices to social organization and mythology. Many of these men became Maximilian's friends and their conversations often lasted late into the night, carried on with the help of Kipp as an interpreter and with Maximilian's growing knowledge of sign language.

While Maximilian recorded verbal data Bodmer executed dozens of studies of villages, dances, and especially people. Reactions to the portraits were varied. One young man, enraged by a snide remark that everyone else had been pictured in his best clothing while he appeared meanly dressed, forced Bodmer to destroy his portrait—but not before the artist secretly made a copy. Another man feared that a portrait might be used magically against him and affect his success in battle. On the whole, however, there was keen interest in all the pictures. Kiäsax, a Piegan Blackfeet man living with the Hidatsa, was especially pleased to see the portraits of his tribesmen done at Fort McKenzie.

In March Maximilian became ill, a seriously swollen leg curtailing his activities. Nonetheless, "during the tedium of my confinement to bed, I was enlivened by the frequent visits of the Indians, and I never neglected to continue my journal, which, from fever and constant weakness, was often very fatiguing." His condition deteriorated and in early April there was concern for his life. The fort's cook was familiar with the symptoms of scurvy, having once seen the disease devastate a garrison at a Missouri River post. Men were cured there by gathering the early green herbs of the prairie, especially the wild onion. "I was advised to make trial of this recipe, and the Indian children accordingly furnished me with an abundance of this plant and its bulbs . . . ." His recovery was speedy and, with the river now completely free of ice, Maximilian's Mackinaw boat was made ready for departure to St. Louis. On the 18th of April gifts and farewells were exchanged, "some cannon-shot were fired by the Fort [as a salute], and we glided rapidly down the beautiful stream of the Missouri."

They arrived in St. Louis about six weeks later. Sturdy new crates for the collections and cages for the bears were ordered and, after a brief reunion with friends, the party left St. Louis for New Harmony. Since reports indicated that the cholera had abated somewhat, the remaining journey to the east coast was planned so that Maximilian could visit places he had missed the year before. Traveling overland and by river and canal, they went from Vincennes to Cincinnati, Cleveland, and Buffalo. Along the way Maximilian continued to pursue his studies in botany and zoology as tirelessly as ever, while Bodmer sketched points of interest such as Niagara Falls. Near Buffalo and below Syracuse on the Erie Canal, the Prince visited settlements of Seneca, Tuscarora, Onondaga and Oneida Indians, four of the six tribes of the "once powerful" Iroquois alliance. At Albany on July 5 they took a Hudson River steamer for New York, and spent the subsequent ten days attending to business in that city and in Philadelphia. On July 16, a little over two years since their arrival in Boston, the three men set sail from New York harbor for Europe and home.

* * * * *

After returning to Europe, Maximilian refined his field notes and transferred them into a three-volume journal of the expedition. From this he prepared a shorter account for publication and contracted with Bodmer to supervise the production of an accompanying set of illustrations. *Reise in das Innere Nord-America in den Jahren 1832 bis 1834* appeared in 1839, followed later by French and English editions, the latter somewhat abridged in translation. Eighty-one aquatints engraved from Bodmer's original works were issued separately between 1839-41, first in portfolio and later bound as the series was completed. Some sets of these black and white prints were hand-colored.

Maximilian and Bodmer collaborated on another project in 1865, the publication of a catalogue of North American reptiles and amphibians, which Bodmer illustrated with engravings. Two years later the Prince died. Bodmer was by then a resident of Barbizon, a compatriot of such painters as Millet and Corot. He was a moderately successful illustrator, and his European landscapes and animal studies were exhibited several times at the Paris Salon. The North American expedition, undertaken in his early twenties, was in retrospect the most significant event in Bodmer's long career. Yet after his association with the Prince ended he never again painted a North American subject. He died in Paris in 1893.

SELECTED BIBLIOGRAPHY

Maximilian, Prince of Wied. Unpublished North American travel journals and related correspondence. Translated typescript by Dr. Emery C. Szmrecsanyi. Center for Western Studies, Joslyn Art Museum.

_____. *Reise in das Innere Nord-America in den Jahren 1832 bis 1834.* Koblenz: J. Hoelscher, 1839-41.

_____. *Voyage dans l'interieur de l'Amérique du Nord exécuté pendant les années 1832, 1833, et 1834,* 3 vols. Paris: Arthus Bertrand, 1840-43.

_____. *Travels in the Interior of North America.* Translated by H. Evans Lloyd. London: Ackermann & Company, 1843.

Maximilian, Prince of Wied's, Travels in the Interior of North America. Early Western Travels, 1748-1846, vols. XXII-XXV. Ed. Reuben Gold Thwaites. Cleveland: Arthur H. Clark Company, 1906.

34.
Máhchsi-Karéhde (Flying War Eagle), Mandan Man
Karl Bodmer
Watercolor on paper
The InterNorth Art Foundation/
Joslyn Art Museum

Maximilian referred to Máhchsi-Karéhde, whose height was just over six feet, as the tallest Mandan. He was a member of the Soldier Society, a group of seasoned warriors that regulated the important affairs of the tribe.

An Appreciation
of Karl Bodmer's Pictures
# of Indians

by John C. Ewers

35.
**Addíh-Hiddísch (Maker of Roads),
Hidatsa Chief**
Karl Bodmer
Watercolor on paper
The InterNorth Art Foundation/
Joslyn Art Museum

Addíh-Hiddísch was one of Maximilian's principal sources of information on the Hidatsa. He was a chief with an impressive war record and, according to Alfred W. Bowers, was still remembered by the Hidatsa a hundred years later as an outstanding leader (*Hidatsa Social and Ceremonial Organization,* Smithsonian Institution, Bureau of American Ethnology Bulletin 194 [1965]: 375).

No other primitive peoples have stirred the interest and imagination of the civilized world as have the North American Indians of the Great Plains Their striking physical appearance and picturesque costumes, their prowess as warriors, horsemen, and big game hunters, and their dramatic dances and religious ceremonies made them especially attractive to artists. Scores of European and American artists sought to interpret graphically the essential attributes of Plains Indian life before the buffalo were exterminated, intertribal warfare terminated, and these Indians were placed upon reservations. One of the first of those artist-interpreters was Karl Bodmer. He was uniquely successful in his efforts.

It is true that a year before Bodmer ascended the Missouri River in 1833 an amazingly energetic American artist, George Catlin, spent a summer in the Indian country of the Upper Missouri. Catlin dedicated his life to recording in words and pictures the appearance and customs of Indian tribes who lived beyond the frontier of white settlement before they and their cultures were destroyed or irrevocably changed through contacts with whites. Working alone, but relying upon fur traders to provide him introductions to the Indians, George Catlin in one short season painted likenesses of prominent tribal leaders and scenes in Indian life among the same tribes Bodmer was to meet in 1833-34. At the same time Catlin gathered information for the greater part of the text of a large, profusely illustrated two-volume book, *Letters and Notes on the Manners, Customs, and Condition of the North American Indians* which he published in London in 1841.

To accomplish so much in a single summer Catlin had to work very quickly. Many of his paintings of Indians were impressionistic—omitting or merely approximating the details of his sitters' costumes or of Indian actions in their villages, in their camp movements, or on their hunts or war expeditions.

On the other hand Karl Bodmer, traveling with the thorough German scientist, Maximilian, Prince of Wied, was able to spend nearly an entire year in the Indian country of the Upper Missouri. Under contract to the Prince to execute field drawings which would illustrate the Prince's written observations during their exploration, Bodmer was free to concentrate most of his time and efforts to that activity. Slowly and painstakingly he compiled his pictorial record, sometimes devoting several days to create a portrait from life of an elaborately clothed chief or prominent warrior. He aimed to make his pictures as detailed and as factual as were the Prince's verbal observations. And Prince Maximilian's journal repeatedly praised Bodmer's renderings of Indians for their accuracy.

We may never know how much the Prince's exacting demands influenced Bodmer's choices of subjects and precision in execution. It is certain this artist pictured only what he saw. He was never content to approximate the details of the subjects he attempted—whether the features of an Indian face, the pattern of a face painting or a body tattoo, the size and shape of a hair, ear or neck ornament, or the furnishings of an Indian earth lodge. As a portrayer of the Indians of the Upper Missouri and their customs Karl Bodmer ranks as the realist *par excellence.*

It would be a grave and romantic mistake to think that the Indians whom Bodmer pictured in 1833 and 1834 were living in or near an aboriginal condition. Most of the tribes of this region had had some contact with white traders for a century or longer before Bodmer met them. Through Indian intermediaries they began to

36.
A Blackfoot Indian on Horse-back
After Karl Bodmer
Engraving with aquatint; hand-colored
The InterNorth Art Foundation/
Joslyn Art Museum

acquire horses and some useful items of European manufacture *even before* they met white men. Even the Blackfeet in the shadow of the Rocky Mountains had acquired horses from the Spanish Southwest and were using them skillfully in hunting buffalo when the first white explorers entered their territory from the east during the mid-eighteenth century. By Bodmer's time some enterprising Blackfeet had accumulated herds of 100 or more horses through raiding enemy camps and breeding their own stock. Possession of pack horses not only enabled the nomadic tribes to use and transport larger and more commodious tipis, they relieved their women of the burden of carrying heavy loads when camp was moved.

Recent archaeological investigations have revealed that farther down the Missouri in the present Dakotas prehistoric Indians constructed more permanent villages of earth-covered lodges fortified with wooden palisades, and that these Indians raised crops of corn, beans and squash in the fertile river bottoms. These villages, occupied by the ancestors of the Mandan, Hidatsa, and Arikara Indians, were important centers of intertribal trade before their residents met white men. When the French trader, Pierre Gaultier de Varennes de la Verendrye, in company with a trading party of Assiniboin, visited the Mandan villages during the winter of 1738-39 he witnessed a lively trade between the sedentary villagers and parties of nomadic Indians in which the former exchanged corn and other garden produce for the dressed skins and products of the chase offered by the nomads. He observed that the Assiniboins, who had obtained goods of European origin directly from French and British traders farther north, brought some of those items to trade with the Mandans. Verendrye reported that those Mandans "are sharp traders and clean

the Assiniboin out of everything they have in the way of guns, powder, ball, knives, axes and awls."[1]

During the last decades of the eighteenth century—before any white men's trading posts were built on the Upper Missouri—the major trading companies farther north sent a few white men to live among the Mandans and Hidatsas, and to serve as their agents in inducing those Indians to furnish beaver pelts and other valuable furs for their northern markets. One of those men was Toussaint Charbonneau, whom Lewis and Clark found living among the Hidatsas during the winter of 1804-05 and who served as interpreter for the American explorers during their explorations westward to the shores of the Pacific Ocean and their return in 1805-06. Charbonneau was an old man still living among the Hidatsas in 1833, and it was this historic personage who introduced Prince Maximilian and Karl Bodmer to the Hidatsas in the fall of that year, an event Bodmer memorialized in his illustration, *The Travellers Meeting with Minatarre Indians near Fort Clark* (Plate 2). In this picture the artist showed himself as the dapper young man in the high hat at the far right. Next to him stands his shorter, more rotund, middle-aged employer, Prince Maximilian. Between them and the group of Indians on the left is redoubtable old Charbonneau gesturing toward the pale-faced visitors as he makes his introductions.

Another of Bodmer's works, *A Blackfoot Indian on Horse-back,* clearly illustrates some of the ways the life of the Indian tribes of the Upper Missouri had been modified by influences from the Old World by Bodmer's time (Plate 36). This Indian of the early 1830s travels on horseback, and is armed with a muzzle-loading gun, probably made in far-off England. He has come a long way from the plodding footman, armed with a lance or bow and arrow, who would have typified the fighting man of his tribe a century earlier. Observe, however, that this man also carries a bow and arrows in a quiver on his back, for that noiseless weapon still was preferred to the loud-mouthed gun as a hunting weapon. His shirt, leggings, and moccasins, are made of animal skins readily available in his own country, although his saddle cloth of mountain lion pelt appears to have been backed with a red strouding obtained from whites in trade.

Had Bodmer traveled up the Missouri as few as three years earlier he probably would not have had an opportunity to picture the Blackfeet Indians, for they were hostile to American fur traders at that time. This animosity had its beginning when Meriwether Lewis, while searching for the sources of the Marias River, a northern tributary of the Missouri just east of the Rockies near the present northern boundary of Montana, met a small party of Piegan Blackfeet, and could not avoid spending the night with them. At dawn next morning the Indians tried to steal the Lewis party's guns and horses. In the ensuing skirmish two of the Indians were killed. That was in July 1806. For a quarter century thereafter the three Blackfeet tribes were bitter and implacable enemies of American traders and trappers. They gave no quarter to aggressive white trappers who sought to take beaver from the streams in their hunting grounds near the Rockies without offering them any recompense. Many lives were lost on both sides during those years, and the Blackfeet twice chased all American trappers out of the present Montana region.

Not until after the St. Louis-based American Fur Company established its most remote upriver post of Fort Union at the mouth of the Yellowstone in 1828 did

37.
Pioch-Kiäiu (Distant Bear), Piegan Blackfeet Man
Karl Bodmer
Watercolor on paper
The InterNorth Art Foundation/ Joslyn Art Museum

38.
Tátsicki-Stomíck (Middle Bull),
Piegan Blackfeet Chief
Karl Bodmer
Watercolor on paper
The InterNorth Art Foundation/
Joslyn Art Museum

Although Tátsicki-Stomíck is
shown here in everyday clothes,
most of the important individuals
painted by Bodmer posed for him
in elaborate native finery. Many of
the chiefs also had fancy uniforms,
plumed felt hats and other articles
of European clothing, gifts given
by the fur companies to secure their
loyalty. These costumes pleased
the Indians, but Maximilian considered the foreign clothing out-
landish and preferred to have
people pictured in native dress.

39.
Stomíck-Sosáck (Bull's Back Fat),
Blood Blackfeet Chief
Karl Bodmer
Watercolor on paper
The InterNorth Art Foundation/
Joslyn Art Museum

Stomíck-Sosáck was about fifty-
years old at the time this portrait
was done at Fort McKenzie. A
silver peace medal, given to him in
recognition of his importance as a
chief, is suspended from a beaded
cord around his neck. Maximilian
noted that the medal bore the
image of President Jefferson;
Bodmer portrayed the obverse,
showing the traditional clasped
hands, tomahawk and pipe.

40.
Fort MacKenzie, August 28th, 1833
After Karl Bodmer
Engraving with aquatint; hand-colored
The InterNorth Art Foundation/
Joslyn Art Museum

American traders open peaceful trade with the dread Blackfeet. That post was in the country of the Assiniboins, eastern neighbors and enemies of the Blackfeet, but its factor, Kenneth McKenzie, was ambitious to extend his trade westward to the Blackfeet. During the fall or winter of 1830 he sent a small party headed by Jacob Berger, an experienced Hudson's Bay Company trader who had known the Blackfeet and spoke their language, to try to induce Blackfeet to come with him to Fort Union. Berger succeeded in bringing about 100 Piegans in to the fort. McKenzie welcomed them with presents and promised to build a trading post in their country the following fall. James Kipp did that, but when he took the first winter's collection of furs downstream the next spring, his employees refused to remain in that exposed location in the country of the feared Blackfeet. So Kipp had to abandon this first American post in Blackfeet country in the spring of 1832, and soon thereafter Indians burned it.

During the early summer of 1832 George Catlin painted the earliest known portraits of Blackfeet Indians who were visiting Fort Union. But Karl Bodmer was the first white artist to observe and picture Blackfeet Indians in their own country, while he and Prince Maximilian resided for five weeks at newly established Fort McKenzie near the mouth of the Marias River during parts of August and September 1833. An atmosphere of cautious, uneasy friendship between whites and Blackfeet prevailed during that period, as the officials of the fur company sought to woo a share of the trade of the Blackfeet away from those Indians' longtime friends, the Hudson's Bay Company north of the international line. Taking advantage of the opportunity, the Prince conducted scientific observations in that locality and Bodmer pictured from life nearly a score of Blackfeet leaders—most of whom probably were avowed enemies of the Americans as recently as two years earlier.

Most of Bodmer's Blackfeet subjects were men of prominence and distinction politically or religiously. They were chiefs or medicine men, many of them beyond middle age. Bodmer took pains to detail the different patterns of face paint worn by his sitters, and the distinctive hairdos of the medicine pipe men which included a topknot of hair wrapped in a leather thong and extended upward and forward from the wearer's forehead. Wearing such a hairdress and a liberal use of blue face paint, with a touch of Chinese vermillion below each eye, the elderly Piegan, Distant Bear, made a striking figure despite his abnormally long chin (Plate 37).

Bodmer obtained likenesses of the principal chiefs of both the Piegan and Blood tribes of Blackfeet. The Piegan head chief, Middle Bull, a courageous old warrior, posed in his ordinary clothes—a skin shirt decorated only with narrow bands of blue and white beadwork over each shoulder. He too wore blue face paint with red touches around his eyes and on his lips (Plate 38). The Blood head chief apparently preferred red. He painted his face a solid red, and wore a shirt of red trade cloth with painted buckskin sleeves and narrow shoulder bands of blue and white beads (Plate 39). He was the only Blackfeet chief to have been portrayed by both Catlin and Bodmer.

What probably was then the height of fashion in Blackfeet women's dress is shown in Bodmer's watercolor of a Piegan young woman, clad in a long dress of skins decorated with narrow bands of blue and white embroidering beads and pendants of larger beads strung on skin cords. Her leggings and moccasins are embroidered in beads of the same colors. Although Bodmer did not name her, this subject was probably a young woman of a wealthy family (Plate 27).

Shortly after dawn on the morning of August 28, 1833 Bodmer had a unique opportunity to see the vaunted Blackfeet fighting men in action. Awakened by the sound of gunfire, the Prince and the painter at first feared the trading post of Fort McKenzie was being attacked. But later from the elevated walkway behind the palisade they plainly saw that the attacking force of some six hundred Assiniboin and Cree Indians was trying to wipe out a band of eighteen or twenty lodges of Piegans camped just outside the fort. Members of that little trading party had been drinking and singing most of the night and had fallen asleep toward morning. Before they could rouse themselves and retreat within the safety of the fort, their surprise attackers ripped open their lodges with knives, discharged their guns and arrows, and killed or wounded a number of men, women and children.

Strengthened by Indian reinforcements from nearby camps and aided by white hunters from the trading post, the Piegans managed to drive the enemies back to the Marias. A fire fight continued until late afternoon and as evening approached the Assiniboins and Crees withdrew toward the Bear Paw Mountains. Head Piegan chief Middle Bull had been a leader in this battle. After the action ended old Bear

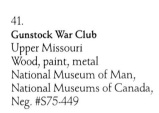

41.
Gunstock War Club
Upper Missouri
Wood, paint, metal
National Museum of Man,
National Museums of Canada,
Neg. #S75-449

This club, formerly in Prince Maximilian's personal collection, was presumably acquired by him on the 1832-34 expedition. Gunstock clubs, so named because the handle resembles the overall shape of a gun, were said by Maximilian to be common among the tribes he observed on the upper Missouri. This one is painted red with a yellow border and floral motifs, and is studded with brass tacks. The blade is double-edged iron.

Chief bragged that "no ball had touched him; doubtless because Mr. Bodmer had taken his portrait a few days before."[2]

From his recollections of this battle and his knowledge of the details of Blackfeet and Assiniboin objects Bodmer developed a very realistic picture of an early phase in the action which appeared over the title *Fort MacKenzie, August 28th, 1833* as an illustration in the atlas which accompanied the Prince's report of their travels. It vividly depicts the ferocity of the action and shows how a variety of weapons were employed: traditional bows and arrows; war clubs; metal-bladed trade knives, one of which, fitted with a bear jaw for a handle, must have been wielded by a man who possessed bear power; and flintlocks. This remains the most accurate and dramatic portrayal of an intertribal battle by a white artist who had witnessed the action (Plate 40).

Some days later Bodmer sketched the great camp of Piegans, totaling about four hundred lodges, pitched close together because they believed the enemy was still near, on the flat near Fort McKenzie. This panorama, with the addition of many foreground figures, was developed into a fine engraving titled *Encampment of the Piekann Indians* appearing in Maximilian's atlas (Plate 42). Unlike many other artists who pictured the camps of nomadic Plains Indians, Bodmer was careful to show tipis of different sizes, reflecting differences in family size and wealth. Newlyweds with no children needed only a small tipi with a cover made from as few as six or eight buffalo cow skins carefully trimmed and fitted together and stretched over a conical framework of relatively short poles. But the family of a wealthy man who had several wives and a large number of children needed several larger tipis of fourteen or more skins each. An experienced trader-observer of the Blackfeet in buffalo days stated, "It is a fine sight to see one of those big men among the Blackfeet, who has two or three lodges, five or six wives, twenty or thirty children, and fifty to a hundred horses; for his trade amounts to upward of $2,000 a year."[3] Such men loaned horses to poor families and secured the services of ambitious young men to help them in hunting. Bodmer's panorama of the large Piegan encampment near Fort McKenzie may have been the most accurate portrayal of a sizable gathering of Plains Indians before the development of photography.

Even though Bodmer spent a longer time among the Blackfeet than among any of the other nomadic tribes of the region he pictured none of their elaborate medicine bundle rituals. This may have been due in part to the fact that Jacob Berger, Prince Maximilian's interpreter among the Blackfeet, professed little interest in the Indians' religion. Also the visitors from abroad probably reached the Blackfeet Country too late in the summer to have witnessed their major tribal religious ceremony of the sun dance, which probably was observed at a site some distance away from the bustling trading post of Fort McKenzie.

In the vicinity of other trading posts farther down the Missouri Bodmer met and pictured members of other nomadic tribes such as the Sioux, Assiniboin, and Cree. On June 1, 1833 he witnessed a group of Sioux racing their horses and one of his engravings in Maximilian's atlas bears the title *Horse Racing of Sioux Indians near Fort Pierre* (Plate 44). While at Fort Union that fall he had an opportunity to take part in a buffalo chase on horseback, and that experience probably helped him to

42.
Encampment of the Piekann [Piegan] Indians
After Karl Bodmer
Engraving with aquatint; hand-colored
The InterNorth Art Foundation/ Joslyn Art Museum

create a lively picture of Indians chasing buffalo which appeared as another illustration in the atlas (Plate 45). The nomadic tribes of the Great Plains depended so much upon the buffalo for food, clothing and shelter, and found so many ingenious uses for its various parts for other purposes that this animal deserved to be looked upon as their staff of life. Illustrative of the Prince and his painter's concern for all aspects of Plains Indian culture are Bodmer's several sketches of a more sombre theme—their methods of burying the dead. Indeed, one of his most elaborate watercolors, *Assiniboin Burial Scaffold,* depicts the bodies of Indians placed upon wooden platforms in trees near Fort Union (Plate 43).

If Bodmer was lucky to have visited the Upper Missouri just late enough to have met the Blackfeet on friendly terms, he was equally lucky to have seen the Mandans before an epidemic of the smallpox reached their villages near Fort Clark by way of the trader's steamboat and which more than decimated that remarkable tribe. During a brief visit to the Mandans in the summer of 1832 Catlin had had the good fortune to observe and to picture their principal religious ceremony of the Okipa which was very rich in drama and symbolism. As the second and the last artist to picture the Mandans and their neighbors the Hidatsas before that tragic plague, Bodmer spent the entire winter of 1833-34 at Fort Clark, within walking distance of the Mandan and Hidatsa villages. James Kipp, the factor at that post, spoke Mandan very well. He introduced Maximilian and Bodmer to those Indians and served as their interpreter.

The largest of the two Mandan villages stood atop a steep bluff on the west bank of the Missouri only 300 paces northwest of Fort Clark. Bodmer's magnificent view of this village, protected by its surrounding log palisade, shows some Mandan women with some of the tub-like bullboats—made by stretching a large buffalo hide over a framework of willows—which those women used to cross the river and make short trips by water during most of the year when the river was not frozen over (Plate 46). This village on the bluff was occupied through all but the coldest months of the year during which these Indians moved into a group of smaller lodges huddled together among the trees of the river bottom. One of Bodmer's field sketches shows in closer view the exterior shapes of the earth lodges, with their long, covered log-framed entrances (Plate 47).

One of Bodmer's masterpieces was a meticulously detailed view of the spacious interior of one of those lodges. It reveals the lodge's basic construction pattern—with four large center posts supporting stringers which in turn hold slanting roof poles covered on the outside with earth, providing a snug interior that was cool in summer. Underneath the open central skylight sit the occupants of this lodge on buffalo robes spread upon the dirt floor. They are surrounded by their useful possessions. In the distance on the left side of the lodge are tied the family's horses. On the floor of that same side are a round, wooden mortar set into the dirt floor and a heavy wooden pestle used by women for grinding corn, beside an inverted basket of the kind women used for harvesting crops and carrying other loads on their back, supported by straps over their chests. Another basket hangs from a peg on the foremost post on the left along with a wooden paddle used for propelling bullboats. At the bottom of that post is one of the clay cooking pots fashioned and used by women. Leaning against the post in the right foreground are men's weapons—lances with sharp blades of metal, and a circular shield comprising a thick base of tough buffalo rawhide, covered with one or more thicknesses of buckskin. On another post at the far right are hung other weapons and ceremonial gear of the lodge owner, including a headdress of buffalo hide with the horns. The engraving of this subject, published under the title *The Interior of the Hut of a Mandan Chief,* is one of the most satisfying pictures of an Indian subject I have seen. Artistically, it is a superb study in light and shadow. Historically and ethnologically it is a remarkably informative pictorial document, filled with revealing details of Mandan lifeways only four years before the terrible smallpox epidemic of 1837 (Plate 48). The Prince tells us that Bodmer spent many days in the lodge of their Mandan informant, Dipäuch, making studies for this view.

That winter of 1833-34 was one of the most severe on record at Fort Clark. The Missouri River froze solid in late November and soon thereafter the Prince observed that there was much activity "on the frozen river, as the Indians are continually going back and forth from their winter to their summer villages, and to the fort. Men, women, children, and dogs dragging little sledges, are seen on it all day long."[4]

Bodmer's distant view of Fort Clark pictures this cold weather activity admirably. The view across the river from the east side shows Fort Clark and the largest of the Mandan villages on the high bluff that forms the west bank. Many people are

43.
Assiniboin Burial Scaffold
Karl Bodmer
Watercolor on paper
The InterNorth Art Foundation/
Joslyn Art Museum

crossing the river on the ice in the middle distance. The men, women, and a child in the foreground are tightly wrapped in buffalo robes. An impression of extreme cold may be gained from the stances of the horse and dog as well (Plate 49).

The quarters provided to the Prince and Bodmer at Fort Clark also served as the artist's studio where he executed portraits of numerous Mandan and Hidatsa Indians who visited the fort. The subzero cold penetrated cracks in the walls of this room and Bodmer's colors sometimes froze so that he could not use them without thawing them out. Despite these inconveniences Bodmer managed to execute a series of exquisitely detailed portraits of selected members of both tribes.

During their winter at Fort Clark the Europeans also witnessed at the fort or in neighboring Indian villages dramatic performances of a number of Indian dances such as they had not been privileged to see in the camps of the Blackfeet the previous summer. One of these was an Hidatsa scalp dance in which the wives of successful warriors carried the enemy scalps their husbands had taken dangling from the ends of long poles (Plate 50). In another dance they saw the elderly women of the White Buffalo Cow Society of the Mandans move in more dignified fashion wearing headbands made from the fur of the sacred white buffalo (Plate 54).

They had repeated opportunities to see dances by members of both Mandan and Hidatsa men's military societies that winter. Of course Bodmer could not draw all the performers in detail and in action, but he did make very precise static renderings of principal participants in their distinctive costumes and quick sketches of groups in action as references in developing pictorial interpretations of some of these dances as illustrations for Maximilian's atlas.

During March 1834 the Hidatsa chief Péhriska-Rúhpa (Two Ravens) spent several days in Bodmer's makeshift studio posing for his portrait arrayed in the elaborate costume he wore as a leader in the dance of one of the most active of his tribe's warrior societies, the Dogs. He wore a huge headdress of owl, magpie, and raven feathers. An eagle bone whistle hung from his neck by a buckskin cord, while a lengthy trailer of red cloth looped around his neck fell down his back. His torso and arms were bare, but he carried in his right hand a rattle made of a curved stick a foot and a half long with animal hoofs fastened to it and an eagle feather pendant at the end. In his left hand he grasped a bow and arrows. Bodmer's original watercolor of this subject was good (Plate 51), but it was further improved in reworking it for publication as an engraving (Plate 52). The action of the dancer was dramatically intensified by bending the body forward, opening the man's mouth, and showing the figure at full length with legs and feet in motion. The entire figure was enriched by a more realistic rendering of well-muscled arms and right shoulder, and detailing of handsomely decorated leggings and moccasins. It is more realistic than a photograph, for every feather, every element of costume design appears to be in sharp focus. I have long considered this the finest full-length portrait of an Indian I have seen. For more than fifteen years a photograph of this work has hung on the wall of my office opposite my desk.

Bodmer also executed a watercolor portrait of the leader of the Mandan Bull Society wearing a large mask over his head made from the head of a bull buffalo including the horns. Its eye and mouth openings were emphasized by surrounding each of them with rings of shiny tin. In one hand he holds his offensive weapon at

44.
**Horse Racing of Sioux Indians
near Fort Pierre**
After Karl Bodmer
Engraving with aquatint;
hand-colored
The InterNorth Art Foundation/
Joslyn Art Museum

45.
Indians Hunting the Bison
After Karl Bodmer
Engraving with aquatint;
hand-colored
The InterNorth Art Foundation/
Joslyn Art Museum

46.
Mih-Tutta-Hang-Kusch,
Mandan Village
After Karl Bodmer
Engraving with aquatint;
hand-colored
The InterNorth Art Foundation/
Joslyn Art Museum

47.
Mandan Earth Lodges
Karl Bodmer
Pencil on paper
The InterNorth Art Foundation/
Joslyn Art Museum

est—a feathered lance with a sharp, double-edged metal blade; in the other his
large shield of rawhide painted black and decorated with strips of red cloth. The
end of his feathered imitation buffalo tail may be seen to the right of the shield
(Plate 57).

On April 9 Prince Maximilian saw and described the ceremonial dance of the
Mandan Bull Society as follows: "Towards evening, nine men of the band of the
buffalo bulls came to the fort to perform their dance, discharging their guns
immediately on entering. One of them wore the entire buffalo head; the others
had pieces of the skin of the forehead, a couple of fillets of red cloth, their shields
decorated with the same material, and an appendage of feathers, intended to
represent the bull's tail hanging down their backs. They also carried long, elegantly
ornamented banners in their hands."[5] During their dance the masked leader imitated
all the motions and sounds of a buffalo bull, charging and timidly retreating, etc.
The engraved and colored version of this scene published in Maximilian's atlas
depicts him in action with his lance raised (Plate 58). He is distinguished from the
other dancers of his society as much by his bright, yellow-painted body with

48.
The Interior of the Hut of a
Mandan Chief
After Karl Bodmer
Engraving with aquatint;
hand-colored
The InterNorth Art Foundation/
Joslyn Art Museum

49.
Mih-Tutta-Hang-Kusch,
Mandan Village
Karl Bodmer
Watercolor on paper
The InterNorth Art Foundation/
Joslyn Art Museum

transverse black stripes across his arms and legs, as by his grotesque, shaggy buffalo head mask with its shiny tin accents. Bodmer pictured this dance as he had seen it earlier in the center of the largest village of the Mandans. Atop a pole to the left is an image of the Evil Spirit. Fascinated Indian onlookers watch the performance from roofs of nearby earth lodges. In his interpretation of this Mandan Bull Society dance Bodmer may have produced the most dramatic still picture of an Indian dance created by any artist. The late Bernard DeVoto wrote of this illustration: "If we were to be limited to a single picture for imaginative insight into the life of the Plains Indians, this one would serve better than any other ever made."[6]

During the five months they stayed at Fort Clark the German Prince and his Swiss artist-colleague established a very close rapport with Mató-Tópe, or Four Bears, whom Catlin had known and appraised as "the most extraordinary man, perhaps, who lives to this day in the atmosphere of Nature's noblemen."[7] Both Catlin and Bodmer painted this remarkable man twice. Although Bodmer found that Four Bears was most proud of his achievements as a warrior and his possession of the best war record of any man in his tribe, this second chief of the Mandans also excelled in other fields. He was the director of his tribe's most complex and sacred religious ceremony, the Okipa. Maximilian found him a fount of knowledge on the customs of his own people and of the neighboring Arikaras. Four Bears

50.
Scalp Dance of the Minatarres
[Hidatsas]
After Karl Bodmer
Engraving with aquatint;
hand-colored
The InterNorth Art Foundation/
Joslyn Art Museum

repeatedly visited the Europeans in their quarters at the fort. Sometimes he brought other interesting Indians to pose for portraits by Bodmer. Occasionally he stayed overnight, sleeping on the floor near the fireplace. A few days before leaving Fort Union in April 1834, Bodmer made a full-length portrait of his friend, Four Bears, dressed in his finest clothing.

Prince Maximilian wrote in his journal: "The vanity which is characteristic of the Indians induced this chief to stand stock-still for several days, so that his portrait succeeded admirably."[8] Surely Bodmer was inspired to create one of his finest Indian portraits in this visual record of an outstanding chief and war hero wearing a colorful outfit befitting his status and so costly that few other chiefs of his time could have afforded it (Plate 53). His handsome bonnet comprised a cap (probably of skin) covered with red cloth and embellished with flat brass buttons obtained from the traders, surmounted by a pair of cut buffalo horns. This cap was lavishly trimmed with strips of the white winter skins of the weasel or American ermine, and it supported a long trailer of eagle feathers. Warriors of the Upper Missouri tribes admired the weasel because they knew it to be the most aggressive animal in that region. The painted wooden knife attached to his cap symbolized the knife he wrested from the hand of a Cheyenne chief in mortal combat. Four Bears' shirt was a new one of bighorn sheepskin, decorated with bands of brightly dyed

51.
Péhriska-Rúhpa (Two Ravens),
Hidatsa Warrior
Karl Bodmer
Watercolor on paper
The InterNorth Art Foundation/
Joslyn Art Museum

52.
Péhriska-Rúhpa (Two Ravens),
Hidatsa Warrior in the Costume of
the Dog Dance
After Karl Bodmer
Engraving with aquatint;
hand-colored
The InterNorth Art Foundation/
Joslyn Art Museum

Plate 51 is evidently a preliminary
watercolor study for the full figure
portrait, Plate 52, which appeared
in the published atlas of aquatints.

porcupine quills covering its shoulder and arm seams, and long pendants of ermine tails falling from the shoulders. On the neck panel is a large triangular design of red and blue cloth edged with beads. Barely visible over the shoulders are small, painted symbols which doubtless referred to his war deeds. Four Bears' leggings appear to be of red trade cloth, decorated with bands of quillwork over their vertical seams. His feet are encased in handsomely quilled moccasins. In his right hand he holds a feathered lance fitted with a sharp, two-edged metal blade obtained from traders. It was a very useful double-purpose trade item that Indians employed as a lancehead or as a knife blade. Attached to a short handle it was suitable for use as a weapon in hand-to-hand combat and in taking scalps, and heavy enough to cut firewood while on expeditions against enemy tribes. The feather attached transversely to the lancehead probably was a personal medicine. The scalp tied to the shaft doubtless was one of the many Four Bears had taken from the enemies he had killed.

53.
Mató-Tópe (Four Bears),
Mandan Chief
Karl Bodmer
Watercolor on paper
The InterNorth Art Foundation/
Joslyn Art Museum

Throughout their travels on the upper Missouri, Bodmer and his princely employer paid close attention to the clothing Indians wore, and in so doing they found that the garments and ornaments worn by prominent Indians were matters of personal more than tribal preference, and that intertribal borrowing of items and decorative styles was not uncommon. They found the Mandan villages were still important centers for intertribal trade in clothing and ornaments, as they had been three decades before in Lewis and Clark's time, or even a century earlier when La Verendrye was the first white man to visit the Mandans (1738). Thus Maximilian observed that most Mandan and Hidatsa Indians did not wear shirts and that the fancy shirts some of them did wear were obtained from the nomadic tribes farther upriver—the Assiniboin, Sioux, Blackfeet and Crow—"either as presents or in barter."[9]

We should not be surprised then to see that in Bodmer's portrait of Kiäsax (Bear on the Left), this Piegan Indian married to an Hidatsa woman and living with her people was wearing a striped Navajo blanket (Plate 56). Doubtless, it too reached its wearer through an extended network of intertribal trade—passing from the Southwest to the Upper Missouri, from the Navajo to Shoshoni, to Crow, to Hidatsa and the Blackfeet Indian living among them.

Maximilian observed Blackfeet adoption of both clothing and weapons from neighboring tribes. Bodmer had pictured Noapéh (Troop of Soldiers), an Assiniboin warrior, in a handsome skin shirt decorated with a large quilled rosette over his chest (Plate 16). When among the Blackfeet he learned that only in recent years had some Blackfeet borrowed the chest rosette from the Assiniboins. Maximilian also noted that the decorative hair pendants worn by a dandy of Kutenai and Piegan ancestry whom Bodmer pictured, named Makúie-Póka (Wolf's Son or Wolf Child), were adopted from the Hidatsas and Mandans (Plate 55). The long, white tubes were trade items fashioned from the lips of Bahamian conch shells brought to New York as ballast in ships by ingenious New Jersey wampum makers, and sold to whites engaged in the Indian trade.[10]

At the same time the Prince learned that most of the war clubs he saw among the Blackfeet "had been taken from the Flatheads," their nearest neighbors on the west side of the Rocky Mountains, and that the Blackfeet had a special liking for

54.
Dance of the Mandan Women
After Karl Bodmer
Engraving with aquatint;
hand-colored
The InterNorth Art Foundation/
Joslyn Art Museum

Crow shields, either captured in war or given them as presents during those rare intervals when peace existed between these two warring tribes.[11]

The Prince found that both the Blackfeet and Mandans preferred the tobacco pipes of handsome red catlinite which they could obtain through barter with the Sioux. Almost certainly the large pipe bowl with extensive lead inlay held by the Hidatsa chief, Two Ravens, in Bodmer's fine portrait of him, was fashioned by the Sioux from pipestone derived from that famous quarry in Sioux territory far to the eastward—a site now preserved as Pipestone National Monument in southwestern Minnesota (Plate 59).

Bodmer's pictures and Maximilian's observations together throw considerable light upon the transition between the native decorative craft of porcupine quillwork and the use of glass trade beads manufactured in Europe and offered to Indians of this region at all of the trading posts on the Missouri. Although quills were still favored by the maker of Four Bears' exquisite outfit (Plate 53), some of the shirts worn by the Blackfeet were decorated with narrow bands of beads in simple, blocky designs. Bodmer pictured the Mandan warrior, Síh-Chidä (Yellow Feather) wrapped in a buffalo robe decorated with a long, wide band of beadwork interspersed with large beaded rosettes (Plate 61). Prince Maximilian learned that formerly such robe decorations were narrower and were executed in quillwork. "This, however, is now old fashioned, and was worn before the coloured glass beads were obtained in such numbers from the Whites."[12]

Bodmer's portraits of costumed Indians show that the marked preference for two colors of beads—blue and white—noticed by Lewis and Clark a quarter century earlier, still persisted among the tribes of the Upper Missouri during the early thirties. This was in striking contrast to the much larger range of bead colors employed by Indian women of the region a half century later, and after they began to use the smaller-sized embroidering beads known as seed beads. Bodmer's evidence on the earlier preference for blue and white is substantiated by a number of beaded objects from the Upper Missouri tribes preserved in the older museums of this country and abroad and known to have been collected before 1860.

Even though a number and variety of European-made materials were in common use among the tribes of this region in Bodmer's time, we should not forget that Indians controlled the ways in which these materials were employed, so that these articles came to bear an undeniable stamp of Indian ingenuity. Uses made of some European-made objects by these Indians would have surprised their makers, had they seen them. Prince Maximilian found that the Mandans had developed a special ceremony for consecrating their firearms, and though they formerly invited guests to this ceremony by distribution sticks, "now European playing cards are actually sent round for this purpose."[13]

Fortunately for students of Indian art both Maximilian and Bodmer were interested in the Indians' own paintings on the inner surfaces of buffalo robes, which Indians wore with the painted sides exposed during cold weather. The two Europeans were painstaking in describing and picturing these works of Indian art accurately.

Among the tribes of the Upper Missouri there were marked differences between men's and women's paintings. Men painted pictographic records of war deeds on buffalo robes so that those who saw them might know of the wearer's accomplishments even more surely than present-day Americans can appraise a soldier's combat record by the stars on his campaign ribbons. Among the Blackfeet Bodmer portrayed a warrior on whose robe a record of his war deeds was painted in the pictorial shorthand then in vogue among those Indians, known to students as "picture-writing." Obviously the painter was more concerned with communicating the wearer's war record than he was in realistically picturing the people and actions involved. Human figures were but simplified stick figures with featureless circles for heads, and linear necks connected to geometric bodies, while arms and legs were represented, if at all, by single lines. Horses were always pictured in profile, and usually with a single leg front and back, each ending in a hooked hoof. Riders either had no legs or had both legs on the same side of the horse. Care was taken to show trophies taken from enemies in enough detail to distinguish such objects as bows, warclubs, lances or guns (Plate 24).

Hidatsa and Mandan picture-writers seemed a bit more concerned with organizing the events in parallel rows, as Bodmer's copy of an Hidatsa painted robe would suggest (Plate 60). But they too were content to represent humans and horses by simple stick figures.

Men also painted religious symbols on other skin surfaces such as drums, shields, and tipi covers. Near Fort Union Bodmer pictured an Assiniboin tipi which the Prince described as "painted of the colour of yellow ochre, had a reddish brown

55.
**Makúie-Póka (Child of the Wolf),
Piegan Blackfeet Man**
Karl Bodmer
Watercolor on paper
The InterNorth Art Foundation/
Joslyn Art Museum

56.
Kiäsax, Piegan Blackfeet Man
Karl Bodmer
Watercolor on paper
The InterNorth Art Foundation/
Joslyn Art Museum

BISONTANZ DER MANDAN INDIANER

BISON-DANCE OF THE MANDAN INDIANS

DANSE DU BISON DES INDIENS MANDANS

border below, and on each of its sides, a large black bear was painted (something of a caricature it must be confessed), to the head of which, just above the nose, a piece of red cloth, that fluttered in the wind, was fastened, doubtless a medicine"[14] (Plate 14). Probably this bear-painted tipi belonged to a member of the secret Assiniboin Bear Cult, comprised of men who had acquired supernatural bear power in dreams and who used it in doctoring and as a war medicine.

Bodmer also pictured the ceremonial drum of Four Bears. On its rawhide head were painted three stylized buffalo hoofs (Plate 64). Life forms appear on only one of several painted shields pictured by Bodmer. On this Crow shield two flying birds are painted, and the entire skins of two weasels are tied to the face of the shield (Plate 64).

Indian women employed geometric forms in their painting. And they painted some robes worn by men as well as others for women. Bodmer's portrait of the Hidatsa chief, Two Ravens, arrayed in his finest clothes, shows a robe draped over his left shoulder which was painted in a pattern Maximilian described as a "feather cap under the image of the sun."[15] This robe is very like a number of later nineteenth century Sioux and Assiniboin painted robes in museum collections.

It is less easy to discern the pattern of a painted woman's robe worn by a Teton

57.
Leader of the Mandan Buffalo Bull Society
Karl Bodmer
Watercolor and pencil on paper
The InterNorth Art Foundation/
Joslyn Art Museum

58.
Bison-Dance of the Mandan Indians
After Karl Bodmer
Engraving with aquatint;
hand-colored
The InterNorth Art Foundation/
Joslyn Art Museum

Sioux woman whom Bodmer pictured, because significant portions of the painting are not visible in this portrait (Plate 65). I am certain, however, that this was an early example of a pattern I designated "border-and-box" in my study of Plains Indian painting nearly a half century ago.[16] A fine example of this design, collected by the American artist Frank B. Mayer, probably among the Sioux in 1851, is in the collection of the Field Museum of Natural History (Cat. No. 12972).

Although in Bodmer's time these two patterns painted by women were rendered only in two colors, red and black, in addition to a size marking (which appears white in the watercolors), many later examples of robes painted with these designs make use of both blue and yellow in the design.

Women among the Upper Missouri tribes made and painted folded rawhide containers which they used for transporting and storing personal and family possessions. Plate 62 shows Bodmer's watercolor rendering of one of the most common forms of those containers, a rawhide envelope known as a parfleche and sometimes spoken of as an "Indian suitcase." This example, preserved in the collection of the Museum für Völkerkunde in Berlin, was collected among the Sioux, but the painted designs are typically Cheyenne. So we appear to have in this case another example of the exchange in artifacts among the tribes of this region in Maximilian and Bodmer's time.

Maximilian and Bodmer were no more impressed by the art produced by the Indians of the Upper Missouri whom they met than were those Indians by Bodmer's pictures. As had Catlin before him, Bodmer encountered some resistance due to some Indians' fears that they might be harmed by the artist's magic if he pictured them. We can understand that fear a little better if we know that among the Indians of that region the creation of an image of another human could be bad medicine. Some Indians were known to have practiced witchcraft by hastily drawing the image of an enemy in the earth and then slowly and deliberately destroying that image, in the anticipation that the enemy would himself be injured or killed soon thereafter. Bodmer, however, seems to have been able to overcome the reluctance of most Indians when they observed his great talent for creating realistic likenesses. The Blackfeet, whose own art had not developed beyond the picture-writing stage, used the same term for the white men's drawings and their writings of words—a term which translates simply as "made marks." It is not strange that the Prince's interpreter among the Blackfeet should have informed him that those Indians thought Bodmer "could write very well." Bodmer received a similar reaction from the Mandans. They called him "Kawakapuska" which meant "the one who makes pictures." The Swiss artist was not performing an alien or unknown function. The Mandans recognized Bodmer as a drawer of pictures, albeit with his own style, and called him by the appropriate term in their own language.[17]

Two Mandans were even more impressed by Bodmer's talents. They were the second chief, Four Bears, and Yellow Feather, the son of a chief, both of whom had artistic interests and ambitions. Bodmer painted two portraits of Four Bears and one of Yellow Feather. They also watched him as he portrayed other members of their tribe and Hidatsa Indians. At the request of Four Bears, Bodmer painted him a white-headed eagle holding a bloody scalp in its claws. Four Bears painted a pictographic record of a number of his most notable coups on a robe for the Prince.

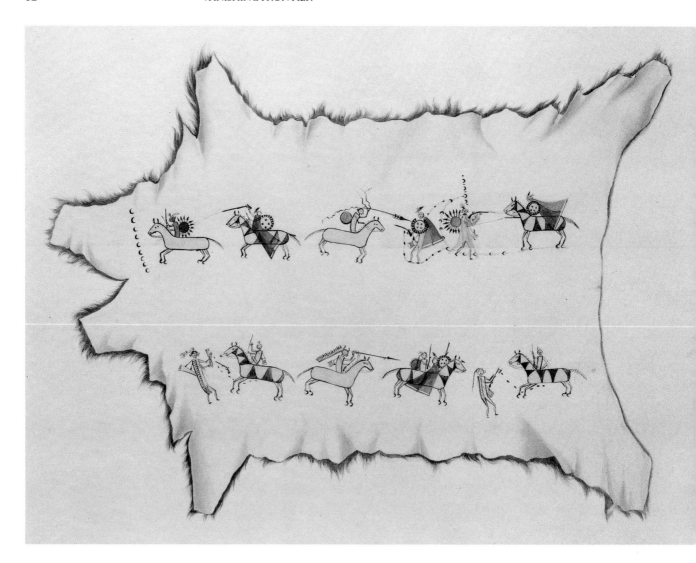

60.
Hidatsa Buffalo Robe
Karl Bodmer
Watercolor on paper
The InterNorth Art Foundation/
Joslyn Art Museum

An inscription on the reverse of this watercolor attributes ownership of the robe depicted to Péhriska-Rúhpa, the Hidatsa warrior shown in Plates 51, 52 and 59. Several battle episodes are portrayed, the protagonist identified by recurring details such as the long, bicolor trailer or scarf.

And finally the Europeans gave both Indians paper, pencils, and watercolors and encouraged them to employ this white man's medium to execute pictures for them. These drawings, preserved in the Joslyn Art Museum, clearly reveal the influence of Bodmer on the art of these two Indians.

Not only did they go about their picture-making in the same way as they had seen Bodmer do it—by first making a precise pencil rendering of their subject, then adding the watercolors—but their works show a marked effort to produce realistically proportioned, fully clothed, human figures with very precisely rendered eyes and other facial features—characteristics completely foreign to traditional Plains Indian picture-writing. One of Four Bears' drawings (Plate 68) portrays his counting of his most significant coup—his killing of a Cheyenne chief in a hand-to-hand combat by taking his enemy's knife from him and killing him with his own weapon. In this very painstaking effort to realistically illustrate that brave action there is even some attempt at color modeling.

Bodmer's influence also shows in Yellow Feather's effort to picture himself on horseback (Plate 69). The style of rendering both man and horse differs greatly from that of the simple figures employed in Plains Indian picture-writing. The

61.
Síh-Chidä (Yellow Feather),
Mandan Man
Karl Bodmer
Watercolor on paper
The InterNorth Art Foundation/
Joslyn Art Museum

This twenty-five year old man was
fascinated by the artwork of both
Maximilian and Bodmer. He asked
them to make drawings for him
and for art supplies of his own, with
which he produced several pictures
like the one shown in Plate 69.

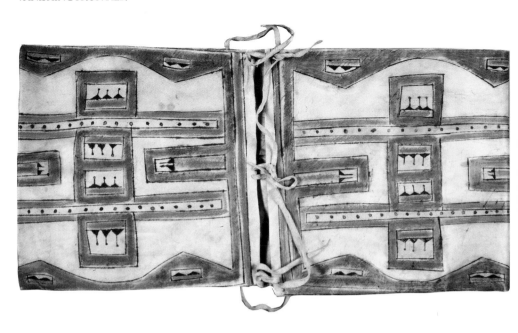

62.
Parfleche
Sioux/Cheyenne
Hide, paint
Courtesy of the Staatliche Museen
Preussischer Kulturbesitz, Museum
für Völkerkunde, Berlin.
Photograph by Gisela
Oestreich.

This rawhide storage container
was collected by Maximilian, who
referred to it as illustrative of Sioux
hide pouches. The design is more
typically Cheyenne, suggesting
that it was a trade item. A faithful
rendering by Bodmer is reproduced
in Plate 63.

rider sits astride his horse. His facial features are indicated in profile and there is a
realistic representation of the human eye. The eye of the horse is rendered with an
equal concern for detail. The ears, nostril, and mouth are delineated. There is some
grace in the entire figure. In contrast to the hooklike hoofs of picture-writing the
hoofs are realistically formed.

Can there be any doubt that this new style of Plains Indian art evidenced by
these works by two Mandan artists in 1834 was inspired, and conditioned by the
example of the young Swiss artist, Karl Bodmer? One of Bodmer's most remarkable
achievements during his sojourn among the Indians of the Upper Missouri was
his service as a missionary of the European tradition of realistic graphic art.[18]

Karl Bodmer's influence upon non-Indian artists of later generations who painted
the Indians of the Plains was most direct upon a young Swiss who was studying
in Paris at the time Bodmer was converting his field sketches into the magnificent
engravings for the atlas which accompanied Prince Maximilian's report of their
travels. Rudolph Friederich Kurz had a romantic interest in picturing redskinned
Apollos and Aphrodites in the American wilderness, but Bodmer prevailed upon
him not to go to the American West until he had perfected his draughtsmanship
to the point where he could record "the prominent characteristics of an object"
with a few swift strokes of his pencil or brush. In mid-century Kurz managed to
secure employment at the forts of the American Fur Company on the upper
Missouri. He was a clerk at Fort Berthold under the supervision of Bodmer's old
friend, James Kipp, during the summer of 1851 when the cholera broke out among
the nearby Hidatsa Indians. Recalling that a destructive smallpox epidemic followed
Catlin and Bodmer's picture-making sojourn among them, the superstitious Indians
pointed to Kurz's drawings as "bad medicine" which was bringing sickness and
death to the red men. So Kurz had to move upstream to Fort Union, where he
filled his sketchbooks with numerous penciled drawings of both Indian and white
traders during the winter of 1851-52. Unpublished for a century thereafter, Kurz's
drawings are now recognized as important pictorial documents on the history

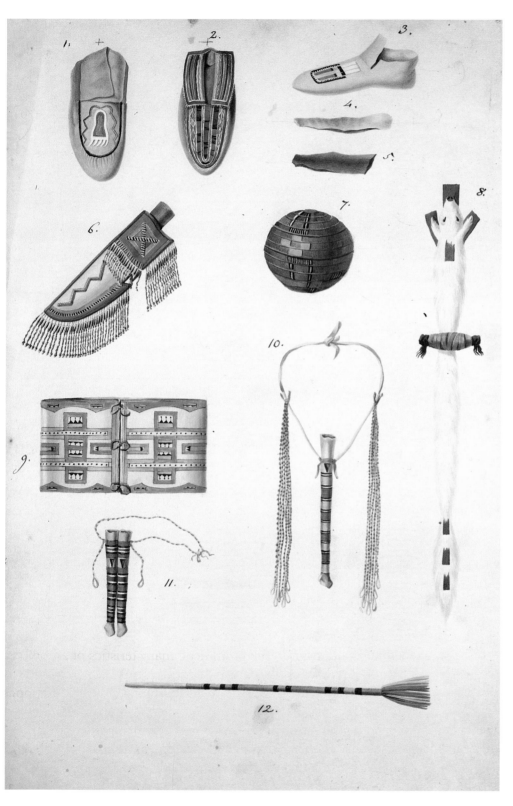

63.
Artifacts
Karl Bodmer
Watercolor and ink on paper
The InterNorth Art Foundation/
Joslyn Art Museum

Evidently a studio work done in
Europe after the journey, this study
depicts several artifacts which were
eventually illustrated in the aquatint atlas. The objects are not drawn
to scale, but Bodmer's attention to
detail can be evidenced by com-
paring Number 9 with the actual
object, shown in Plate 62.

1. Moccasin, Sioux; 2. Moccasin,
Iroquois?; 3. Moccasin, Sioux?;
4. Stone knife, found near New
Harmony, Indiana; 5. Stone knife,
Mexican; 6. Knife and sheath,
Upper Missouri; 7. Ball, Mandan
or Hidatsa; 8. Ermine pouch,
Upper Missouri; 9. Parfleche,
Sioux/Cheyenne; 10.-11. War whis-
tles, Mandan; 12. Pipe tamper,
Assiniboin.

64.
Details from **Indian Utensils and Arms**
After Karl Bodmer
Engraving with aquatint;
hand-colored
The InterNorth Art Foundation/
Joslyn Art Museum

The shield is Crow. The drum
belonged to the Mandan chief
Mató-Tópe.

and ethnology of the Upper Missouri of a generation *after* Bodmer was active in that region.[19]

Other artists learned of Bodmer's pictorial interpretations of the Indians of the Upper Missouri through the superb engravings in the atlas which accompanied Prince Maximilian's *Travels in the Interior of North America*. Even though it was published in German, French, and English editions in the early 1840s, this work was so expensive that few artists in America knew of it unless they had access to the major libraries in the eastern cities. In 1845 *Graham's Magazine* began to offer selected examples of a dozen of the most popular of Bodmer's works in the form of steel engravings of much smaller size than the atlas illustrations. These reproductions in an American magazine were issued at a rate of one picture per issue accompanied by an explanatory text.[20]

By the 1850s it was not uncommon for publishers of popular books about Indians or American history to illustrate them with poorly executed copies of Bodmer's works while attributing the portraits to likenesses of well-known Indian heroes of earlier times among the tribes of the Eastern Woodlands, such as Samoset, the early seventeenth century friend of pioneer English settlers in New England. I have a small book which was adopted as a text on American history for the public schools of Maryland in 1865 in which a small reproduction of Bodmer's Hidatsa Indian dog dancer appears on the first page of a chapter devoted to the Indians at the time of Columbus.[21]

Some of the most dramatic and popular of the Currier and Ives prints published during the 1850s and 1860s were scenes in Plains Indian life—especially actions in buffalo hunting and warfare. They were lithographed from very realistic compos-

65.
Chan-Chä-Uiá-Teüin (Woman of the Crow Nation), Teton Sioux Woman
Karl Bodmer
Watercolor on paper
The InterNorth Art Foundation/
Joslyn Art Museum

The name of this young woman implies a kinship with the Crow tribe. Since the Teton and the Crow were bitter enemies it may be that she was taken as a captive in a raid, or was the daughter of a captive, raised as a Sioux.

66.
**Mató-Tópe (Four Bears),
Mandan Chief**
Karl Bodmer
Watercolor on paper
The InterNorth Art Foundation/
Joslyn Art Museum

There are two portraits of Mató-
Tópe, one showing him in splendid full dress (Plate 53) and this one,
depicting him as a warrior. Mató-
Tópe was said by Maximilian to
have killed more than five chiefs in
intertribal combat, and his heroic
accomplishments were highly
regarded by his people. The yellow
hand on his chest indicates that he
had captured prisoners, and the
barred stripes on his arm represent
other warlike deeds. Among the
coup symbols worn in his hair are
six wooden sticks which symbol-
ize gunshot wounds received in battle, and a wooden knife, a carved
and painted facsimile of the deadly
weapon that he wrested from a
Cheyenne in a fierce struggle—the
same struggle he depicted in
Plate 68.

67.
War Emblems
Mandan
Wood, paint, metal
Courtesy of the Linden-Museum,
Stuttgart. Photograph by Ursula
Didoni.

Plate 66 shows Mató-Tópe
wearing a wooden knife and six
wooden sticks in his hair as symbols of battle accomplishments.
Maximilian asked Mató-Tópe to
duplicate these, which he did, and
Maximilian added them to his
collection. The knife is painted red
with a yellow stripe; the sticks are
various combinations of red, blue
and yellow.

itions executed jointly by German-born Louis Maurer and English-born Arthur
Fitzwilliam Tait, neither of whom left the security of their New York studios to
learn about Indians at firsthand. Maurer acknowledged that he learned about Indians
from the reproductions of Bodmer's and Catlin's works in the Astor Library in
New York City.[22]

Frederic Remington had no knowledge of Bodmer's works until some years after
he had gained a considerable reputation as a pictorial interpreter of the Old West.
Then on January 7, 1892 Francis Parkman, famed author of *The Oregon Trail*, seeking
to help Remington prepare a new series of illustrations for his American classic,
based upon his firsthand experiences among the Sioux and Cheyenne along the
Oregon Trail in 1846, wrote the artist suggesting that Remington consult Karl
Bodmer's illustrations of Indians in Maximilian's atlas. Parkman stated, "He paints
the Indian exactly as . . . I saw them." Two days later Remington enthusiastically
informed Parkman that he had examined Bodmer's works in the Astor Library.
"Before that I had never heard of the book, and I was delighted. Bodmer drew
much better than Catlin and in fact was able to render what he saw to a very fine
account. He was tremendiously [sic] painstaking, and for refference [sic] and scientific
purposes he was much better—even better than a modern man who would give
you more of his heart than he did of his head."[23]

Remington's most talented rival in the pictorial reconstruction of highlights in the history of the Old West was the Montana cowboy-artist, Charles M. Russell. He revealed his high regard for Bodmer's works as a model for his own in his oil painting of a dramatic incident in the history of the Lewis and Clark expedition when an Hidatsa Indian, believing that William Clark's negro slave, York, must have been a white man painted black, wet a finger and tried to rub off some of that coloring. In this 1908 painting, simply titled *York*, Russell renders an earth lodge interior much like Bodmer's classic illustration of a Mandan one. The costumes of the Hidatsa Indians also look like they were derived from Bodmer's illustrations, even to the rendering of the chief seated on the earth lodge floor between Lewis and Clark wearing a copy of the finely detailed feathered headdress pictured in Bodmer's illustration of the dog dancer.[24]

Francis Parkman, known to have possessed a fine collection of Bodmer's prints, surely was not unique among American historians as an admirer of Bodmer's accuracy as a pictorial reporter of Indian life. Frank Weitenkampf, longtime Curator of Prints at the New York Public Library and a serious student of the abilities of artists to picture North American Indians, wrote of Bodmer: "The whole of his drawings for the Prince of Wied's book seem the most convincing pictures of Indians made in his time."[25]

Historians and anthropologists as well as other serious students of Plains Indian history and culture find Bodmer's works to be uniquely significant for their nearly ideal documentation as well as their artistic qualities. Not only are the subjects of most of his original watercolors named and their dates of execution recorded, but the places and circumstances of their creation are further explained in Prince Maximilian's published observations on their travels. For example, we know that on May 26, 1833 at the Sioux Agency of Fort Lookout, Bodmer executed a full-length portrait of the Yankton Sioux warrior, Big Soldier (Plate 11). His name and this date appear on Bodmer's original watercolor of this subject in the collections of the Joslyn Art Museum. Prince Maximilian further states that this Indian "remained the whole day in the position required" while Bodmer with infinite pains drew and painted his portrait. When the work was completed the demanding scientist Maximilian pronounced it a "very capital likeness."[26]

No scholars hold Bodmer's Indian illustrations in higher esteem than do those anthropologists who have devoted many years of their lives to field investigations of the Indian tribes of the Upper Missouri region. One of them was the Army physician, Washington Matthews, who closely studied the Hidatsa Indians still living in earth lodges near the military post of Fort Berthold where he was stationed during the late 1860s. Matthews was also an amateur artist, and he was critical of the way in which George Catlin had pictured Mandan and Hidatsa earth lodges as simple hemispherical, domed structures. Matthews credited Karl Bodmer with "the first truthful pictures ever published" of these ingeniously constructed homes of the Mandan and Hidatsa Indians.[27]

Clark Wissler, head of the Department of Anthropology of the American Museum of Natural History in New York City, carefully studied both the Teton Sioux and the Blackfeet in the field during the first decade of this century. He also supervised the most intensive program for study of the history and ethnology of all of the tribes of the Upper Missouri ever attempted, under the sponsorship of

his museum during the first quarter of this century. Wissler had a very high regard for the accuracy of Karl Bodmer's published illustrations of Indians of the region. The first volume of *The Pageant of America,* a thoroughly researched pictorial history published by Yale University Press, dealt largely with the Indian tribes of North America. Wissler selected and wrote the captions for the pictures of Indians. He chose no fewer than seventeen of Bodmer's works to illustrate the chapter on the Plains Indians.[28] For the frontispiece of his more technical volume on the Indians of the entire western hemisphere, *The American Indian* (1917), Wissler offered a reproduction of Bodmer's classic engraving of the Hidatsa dog dancer.

As my professor at Yale a half-century ago, Clark Wissler first introduced me to Karl Bodmer's pictures of Indians. In my first book, an elaboration of my Masters' Thesis, I referred to Bodmer as "a meticulous draughtsman, with a camera-like eye, who was concerned with the accurate rendering of design details and the quality and texture of materials."[29] As my own studies of Plains Indian art, history, and ethnology have broadened and deepened over the years, my appreciation of the importance of Bodmer's pictures has grown. I have no doubt that Karl Bodmer surpasses all others as the master painter and illustrator of the Plains Indians.

Finally, we should recognize that Bodmer's portraits of Indians have had a very special significance to the descendants of the Indians whom he portrayed a century and a half ago. Bodmer helped to make Four Bears, the Mandan second chief, the best known Indian of his time among the tribes of the Upper Missouri. It was important for his descendants to know what this great chief looked like, for verbal accounts of his achievements were handed down from mouth to ear from generation to generation. In 1930, nearly a century after Four Bear's untimely death in the smallpox epidemic of 1837, an anthropologist heard Indians on the Fort Berthold Reservation in North Dakota tell stories of his heroic deeds on the warpath, and they still honored his memory as a two-time leader in their most sacred tribal ceremony of the Okipa.[30]

More than forty years ago I listened to Weasel Tail, an aged Blood Indian, recite by name the succession of principal chiefs of his tribe back an undetermined number of years totaling more than two centuries. Among them he mentioned Stomíck-Sosáck (Bull's Back Fat), whose portrait Bodmer executed from life at Fort McKenzie in 1833. Some time later Weasel Tail and I leafed through a copy of Prince Maximilian's atlas which I had obtained for the library of the Museum of the Plains Indian on the Blackfeet Reservation, Montana. Weasel Tail pointed to one of the portraits and said "Stomíck-Sosáck." Through our interpreter I asked him what made him think that was the man Bodmer pictured, since I knew the portrait was executed two decades *before* Weasel Tail was born. Weasel Tail replied promptly. "I knew his son. He looked just like that picture."

NOTES

[1]Lawrence J. Burpee, ed., *Journals and Letters of Pierre Gaultier de Varennes de la Verendrye and his Sons* (Toronto: The Champlain Society, 1927), p. 332.

[2]Maximilian, Prince of Wied, *Travels in the Interior of North America 1832-1834*, Reuben Gold Thwaites, ed., *Early Western Travels, 1748-1846*, vols. XXII-XXV (Cleveland: Arthur H. Clark Co., 1906), 23: 146-153.

[3]Charles Larpenteur, *Forty Years A Fur Trader On The Upper Missouri, The Personal Narrative of Charles Larpenteur 1833-1872*, Elliott Coues, ed., 2 vols. (New York: Francis P. Harper, 1898), 2: 401.

[4]Maximilian, *Travels*, 23: 236.

[5]Ibid., 24: 79.

[6]Bernard DeVoto, *Across The Wide Missouri* (Boston: Houghton Mifflin Company, 1947), p. 403.

[7]Geo. Catlin, *Letters And Notes on the Manners, Customs, And Condition of the North American Indians*, 2 vols. (London: Author, 1841), 1: 92.

[8]Maximilian, *Travels*, 24: 79.

[9]Ibid., 23: 161.

[10]Ibid., pp. 99-101.

[11]Ibid., pp. 119, 161.

[12]Ibid., p. 263.

[13]Ibid., p. 342.

[14]Ibid., p. 19.

[15]Ibid., p. 261.

[16]John C. Ewers, *Plains Indian Painting, A Description of an Aboriginal American Art* (Palo Alto: Stanford University Press, 1939), pp. 9-10.

[17]Maximilian, unpublished "Diary of a Journey to North America in the years 1832, 1833, 1834," 3 vols., 3: 138; Robert C. Hollow to Joseph C. Porter, June 23, 1983.

[18]John C. Ewers, "Early White Influence upon Plains Indian Painting: George Catlin and Karl Bodmer among the Mandans, 1832-34," *Indian Life on the Upper Missouri* (Norman: University of Oklahoma Press, 1968), pp. 75-97.

[19]John C. Ewers, *Artists of the Old West* (Garden City: Doubleday & Co., 1965), pp. 137-149.

[20]*Graham's Magazine*, January 1845-September 1850, passim.

[21]Samuel G. Goodrich, *The American Child's Pictorial History of the United States* (Philadelphia: E. H. Butler, 1861), p. 23.

[22]Harry T. Peters, *America on Stone* (Garden City: Doubleday, Doran, & Co., 1931), p. 21.

[23]Wilbur R. Jacobs, ed., *Letters of Francis Parkman*, 2 vols. (Norman: University of Oklahoma Press, 1960), 2: 253-254.

[24]Ewers, *Artists of the Old West*, p. 231.

[25]Frank Weitenkampf, "Early Pictures of North American Indians. A Question of Ethnology," *Bulletin of the New York Public Library*, 53 (1949): 614.

[26]Maximilian, *Travels*, 22: 307-311.

[27]Washington Matthews, "The Earthlodge in Art," *American Anthropologist*, n.s. 4 (1902): 9.

[28]Clark Wissler, Constance Lindsay Skinner, and William Wood, *Adventures in the Wilderness, The Pageant of America*, vol. I (New Haven: Yale University Press, 1925).

[29]Ewers, *Plains Indian Painting*, p. 29.

[30]Alfred W. Bowers, *Mandan Social and Ceremonial Organization* (Chicago: The University of Chicago Press, 1950), pp. 70, 123.

List of Illustrations

Color plates are indicated by an asterisk

Checklist of the Exhibition

ARTWORKS

All artworks are listed alphabetically by title within categories: *Watercolors and Drawings by Karl Bodmer; Aquatints After Karl Bodmer;* and *Works by Other Artists.* Dimensions are in inches; height precedes width. All artworks are from the collection of The InterNorth Art Foundation on permanent loan to the Joslyn Art Museum, Omaha, Nebraska.

Watercolors and Drawings by Karl Bodmer
(1809-1893)

Addih-Hiddísch (Maker of Roads), Hidatsa Chief
Watercolor on paper
16½ x 11⅝

Ahschüpsa-Masihichsi (Chief of the Pointed Horn), Hidatsa Man
Watercolor on paper
12⅛ x 9⅛

Artifacts
Watercolor and ink on paper
16½ x 10⅝

Artifacts
Watercolor and ink on paper
15⅜ x 9⅜

Assiniboin Burial Scaffold
Watercolor on paper
12½ x 9⅞

Assiniboin Camp
Watercolor on paper
7½ x 10⅜

Assiniboin Man
Watercolor and pencil on paper
17 x 11⅞

Assiniboin Medicine Sign
Watercolor on paper
9⅝ x 12¼

Awascho Dickfas (Swallow with the White Belly), Hidatsa Man
Watercolor and pencil on paper
12½ x 10⅛

Backwoods Man and Woman on Horseback
Pencil on paper
6⅜ x 8⅝

Beaver Lodge on the Missouri
Watercolor on paper
7⅞ x 10¾

Bellevue Agency, Post of Major Dougherty
Watercolor on paper
6½ x 9½

Biróhka, Hidatsa Man
Watercolor and pencil on paper
12⅝ x 9⅝

Blackfeet-Assiniboin Girl
Watercolor on paper
10⅝ x 8

Bon Pas on Green's Prairie
Pencil on paper
6¼ x 8⅝

Boston Lighthouse
Watercolor on paper
6⅜ x 8⅝

Buffalo
Watercolor on paper
6⅜ x 8⅝

Buffalo and Elk on the Upper Missouri
Watercolor on paper
9¾ x 12¼

Chan-Chä-Uiá-Teüin (Woman of the Crow Nation), Teton Sioux Woman
Watercolor and pencil on paper
17 x 11⅞

Citadel Rock on the Upper Missouri
Ink wash on paper
12⅜ x 7¾

The Confluence of the Fox River and the Wabash
Watercolor on paper
11⅞ x 14½

Court House at Mount Vernon
Watercolor on paper
6⅜ x 8¾

Cree Woman
Watercolor and pencil on paper
11⅞ x 9⅝

Deck Plan of the Steamboat Homer
Watercolor on paper
6⅜ x 8⅝

Economy, Rapp's Colony on the Ohio
Watercolor on paper
10¾ x 17

Evening Bivouac on the Missouri
Watercolor (sepia wash) and ink on paper
9⅛ x 12⅛

Female Bullfrog
Watercolor and pencil on paper
6⅜ x 8

Figures
Pencil on paper
12⅝ x 10

Fort Adams on the Mississippi
Watercolor on paper
6⅜ x 8⅝

Fort McKenzie at the Mouth of the Marias River
Watercolor on paper
10¾ x 16⅞

Gopher
Wash and ink on paper
10⅝ x 14¾

Head of an Antelope
Watercolor on paper
9¾ x 11⅛

Head of a Crane
Watercolor and pencil on paper
10⅝ x 14⅞

Head of a Female Bighorn Sheep
Watercolor and pencil on paper
10⅝ x 13½

Head of a Vulture
Watercolor on paper
8¾ x 10⅞

Hidatsa Scalp Dance
Watercolor and pencil on paper
10 x 12⅜

Íhkas-Kínne (Low Horn), Siksika Blackfeet Chief
Watercolor and pencil on paper
17 x 11⅞

Interior of a Mandan Earth Lodge
Watercolor and ink on paper
11¼ x 16⅞

Junction of the Yellowstone and the Missouri
Watercolor on paper
10⅜ x 16¾

Kiäsax (Bear on the Left), Piegan Blackfeet Man
Watercolor on paper
12¼ x 9½

Leader of the Mandan Buffalo Bull Society
Watercolor and pencil on paper
16¹⁵⁄₁₆ x 11⅝

Lesueur, The Naturalist at New Harmony
Watercolor on paper
6⅞ x 10⅛

Lynx
Ink, pencil and wash on paper
10½ x 14¾

*Máhchsi-Karéhde (Flying War Eagle),
Mandan Man*
Watercolor and pencil on paper
16⅞ x 12

Máhchsi-Níhka (Young War Eagle), Mandan Man
Watercolor and ink on paper
12¼ x 9⅞

*Makúie-Póka (Child of the Wolf), Piegan Blackfeet
Man*
Watercolor on paper
12¼ x 9⅞

Mandan Buffalo Robe
Watercolor on paper
12 x 16¾

Mandan Dog Sled
Watercolor and ink on paper
7⅞ x 12¼

Mandan Earth Lodges
Pencil on paper
3⅞ x 6

Mandan Pipe
Watercolor on paper
10 x 12½

Mandan Shrine
Watercolor and pencil on paper
8 x 10⅜

Mandan Shrine
Watercolor on paper
10¼ x 7⅞

Mandeh-Kahchu (Eagle's Beak), Mandan Man
Watercolor and pencil on paper
12½ x 10

Mató-Tópe (Four Bears), Mandan Chief
Watercolor on paper
13¾ x 11¼

Mató-Tópe (Four Bears), Mandan Chief
Watercolor on paper
16½ x 11⅝

*Mehskéhme-Sukáhs (Iron Shirt), Piegan Blackfeet
Chief*
Watercolor, ink and pencil on paper
12½ x 10⅛

Mexkemauastan (Stirring Iron), Atsina Chief
Watercolor on paper
16½ x 11¼

Mih-Tutta-Hang-Kusch, Mandan Village
Watercolor on paper
11¼ x 16⅝

Mih-Tutta-Hang-Kusch, Mandan Village
Watercolor and pencil on paper
11⅞ x 16⅞

The Mississippi Near St. Genevieve
Watercolor on paper
4⅞ x 6¾

Mouth of the Big Sioux River
Watercolor on paper
8⅞ x 14¾

Mouth of the Platte River
Watercolor and pencil on paper
10⅝ x 16⅝

Muskrat
Watercolor on paper
9 x 14½

Niätóshä, Atsina Chief
Watercolor and pencil on paper
10 x 12½

Noapéh (Troop of Soldiers), Assiniboin Man
Watercolor and pencil on paper
17 x 11⅞

Ohio-Mississippi River Keelboat
Watercolor on paper
5⅞ x 8½

Ohio River Near Rome
Watercolor on paper
6⅜ x 8⅝

Omaha Boy
Watercolor on paper
10⅞ x 7⅞

Omaha Man
Watercolor and pencil on paper
11⅞ x 8½

Péhriska-Rúhpa (Two Ravens), Hidatsa Man
Watercolor on paper
15⅞ x 11½

Péhriska-Rúhpa (Two Ravens), Hidatsa Man
Watercolor on paper
17 x 11¾

Piegan Blackfeet Man
Watercolor and pencil on paper
12⅜ x 10

Piegan Blackfeet Woman
Watercolor and pencil on paper
17 x 12

Pioch-Kiäiu (Distant Bear), Piegan Blackfeet Man
Watercolor on paper
12⅜ x 10⅛

Pipes
Watercolor and pencil on paper
16⅛ x 10⅛

Pitàtapiú, Assiniboin Man
Watercolor and pencil on paper
16¾ x 11⅞

Ponca Camp
Watercolor on paper
6 x 9¾

Portland on the Ohio
Watercolor on paper
6⅜ x 8⅝

Prince Maximilian in Military Uniform
Pencil on paper
4⅜ x 2⅞

Quiver, Bows and Arrows
Watercolor and pencil on paper
10⅛ x 10⅜

Remarkable Elevations on the Upper Missouri
Watercolor and pencil on paper
12½ x 7⅞

Remarkable Elevations on the Upper Missouri
Watercolor and pencil on paper
12½ x 7⅞

Remarkable Elevations on the Upper Missouri
Watercolor and pencil on paper
12⅛ x 7⅝

Remarkable Elevations on the Upper Missouri
Watercolor and pencil on paper
12¼ x 7⅞

Rock Formations on the Upper Missouri
Watercolor on paper
7⅞ x 12⅜

Scene on the Janus
Watercolor on paper
5½ x 8

Schuh-De-Gá-Che (He Who Smokes), Ponca Chief
Pencil and wash on paper
11¾ x 8⅜

Síh-Chidä (Yellow Feather), Mandan Man
Watercolor on paper
17⅛ x 11⅞

Síh-Sä (Red Feather), Mandan Man
Watercolor on paper
12¼ x 9½

Sioux Camp
Watercolor on paper
7⅝ x 10⅜

Snags on the Missouri River
Watercolor and pencil on paper
8⅝ x 10¾

Snake Woman
Watercolor on paper
12½ x 9⅜

The Steamboat Yellow Stone
Watercolor and pencil on paper
8¼ x 13¼

*Stomíck-Sosáck (Bull's Back Fat), Blood Blackfeet
Chief*
Watercolor and pencil on paper
12⅜ x 9¾

A Stop, Evening Bivouac
Watercolor on paper
10¹/₂ x 9¹/₄

Tátsicki-Stomíck (Middle Bull), Piegan Blackfeet Chief
Watercolor on paper
12¹/₂ x 10¹/₈

Toad
Watercolor on paper
8 x 10

Tsholocha, Cherokee Man
Watercolor and pencil on paper
8⁵/₈ x 6³/₈

Tukán-Hätón (Horned Rock), Yankton Sioux Chief
Watercolor and pencil on paper
16³/₄ x 11⁵/₈

Tulope, Choctaw Man
Watercolor and pencil on paper
8⁵/₈ x 6³/₈

Turtle (Chrysemys picta)
Watercolor on paper
8 x 10

Unidentified Woman
Pencil on paper
12⁵/₈ x 10

Unusual Formations on the Upper Missouri
Watercolor on paper
12¹/₄ x 7³/₄

Unusual Formations on the Upper Missouri
Watercolor and pencil on paper
12¹/₂ x 7⁷/₈

Unusual Formations on the Upper Missouri
Watercolor on paper
10¹/₂ x 7³/₄

Unusual Formations on the Upper Missouri
Watercolor and pencil on paper
12¹/₈ x 7⁵/₈

Upsichtä (Great Blackness), Mandan Man
Watercolor on paper
12¹/₂ x 9⁷/₈

View of Bethlehem on the Lehigh
Watercolor on paper
11⁷/₈ x 17¹/₄

View of Coal Mine Near Mauch Chunk, with Railroad
Watercolor on paper
11⁷/₈ x 17

View of a Farm on the Illinois Prairie
Watercolor on paper
5¹/₄ x 8³/₈

View of Helvoet
Pencil on paper
6³/₈ x 8⁵/₈

View of the Highwood Mountains from Fort McKenzie
Watercolor on paper
11³/₄ x 16⁷/₈

View of the Highwood Mountains from Fort McKenzie
Watercolor on paper
11¹/₂ x 16³/₈

View of New Harmony
Watercolor on paper
6¹/₄ x 10³/₄

View of Niagara Falls
Watercolor on paper
12¹/₄ x 20

View of the Stone Walls
Watercolor on paper
9⁷/₈ x 16⁷/₈

View on the Delaware near Bordentown
Watercolor on paper
11³/₄ x 16³/₄

View on the Missouri, Blackbird Hills
Watercolor on paper
7⁵/₈ x 11¹/₄

Wahktägeli (Gallant Warrior), Yankton Sioux Chief
Watercolor and pencil on paper
16³/₄ x 11⁵/₈

White-Tailed Deer (Odocoileus virginianus)
Pencil and watercolor on paper
10¹/₄ x 14⁷/₈

The White Castles on the Missouri
Watercolor on paper
9 x 16¹/₄

The White Castles on the Missouri
Watercolor on paper
5¹/₈ x 7³/₄

Young Turtle (Graptemys pseudogeographica)
Ink and watercolor on paper
10⁵/₈ x 6¹/₄

Aquatints After Karl Bodmer

Bison-Dance of the Mandan Indians
Engraving with aquatint; hand-colored
16¹/₂ x 21¹/₂

Camp of the Gros Ventres [Atsina] of the Prairies on the Upper Missouri
Engraving with aquatint; hand-colored
13³/₄ x 17¹/₄

Dance of the Mandan Women
Engraving with aquatint; hand-colored
9⁷/₈ x 13

Encampment of the Piekann [Piegan] Indians
Engraving with aquatint; hand-colored
16¹/₄ x 21¹/₂

Fort MacKenzie, August 28th, 1833
Engraving with aquatint; hand-colored
16¹/₄ x 21¹/₂

Fort Pierre on the Missouri
Engraving with aquatint; hand-colored
13³/₄ x 17¹/₄

Fort Union on the Missouri
Engraving with aquatint; hand-colored
13³/₄ x 17

Hunting the Grizzly Bear
Engraving with aquatint; hand-colored
16¹/₂ x 21¹/₂

Indian Utensils and Arms
Engraving with aquatint; hand-colored
16¹/₄ x 21¹/₂

Massika, Saki [Sauk] Indian and Wakusasse, Musquake [Fox] Indian
Engraving with aquatint; hand-colored
15⁷/₈ x 19⁵/₈

Mató-Tópe, Adorned with the Insignia of His Warlike Deeds
Engraving with aquatint; hand-colored
17¹/₄ x 11³/₄

Scalp Dance of the Minatarres [Hidatsa]
Engraving with aquatint; hand-colored
16 x 21¹/₄

Scalp Dance of the Minatarres [Hidatsa]
Engraving with aquatint
16 x 21¹/₄

The Travellers Meeting with Minatarre [Hidatsa] Indians Near Fort Clark
Engraving with aquatint; hand-colored
11¹/₄ x 13³/₄

View of the Stone Walls on the Upper Missouri
Engraving with aquatint; hand-colored
16 x 21

Winter Village of the Minatarres [Hidatsa]
Engraving with aquatint; hand-colored
14¹/₄ x 17¹/₄

Works by Other Artists

Berock-Heddish at Okippe Feast
Síh-Chidä
Watercolor and pencil on paper
6¹/₄ x 4⁵/₈

Drawing
Mató-Tópe
Watercolor and pencil on paper
12³/₈ x 15⁵/₈

Portrait of Prince Maximilian with His Brother Prince Charles
Prince Charles of Wied
Oil on canvas
45¹/₄ x 32

Self-Portrait
Síh-Chidä
Watercolor and pencil on paper
7³/₄ x 12³/₈

ETHNOGRAPHIC AND HISTORIC OBJECTS

Objects are listed by lenders in alphabetical order. Dimensions are given in inches for maximum measurements.

American Museum of Natural History, New York, New York

Necklace, Atsina
Fur, hide, bear claws, cloth, beads, ribbon
Length 22
Cat. no. 50/4276
Collected by C. Wissler at Fort Belknap in 1903.

Basket, Hidatsa
Splints, wood, hide
Diameter 16½
Cat. no. 50/7174
Collected by G. Wilson in 1908; made by Buffalo Bird Woman.

Headdress, Mandan
Hide, feather, wood
Width 24
Cat. no. 50.1/5374
Collected by G. Wilson at Fort Berthold in 1909.

Flute, Sioux
Wood, feather, hide, ribbon
Length 20
Cat. no. 50.1/7316
Collected by C. Nines at Pine Ridge in 1913.

The Brooklyn Museum, Brooklyn, New York

Knife and Knife Sheath, Sioux
Hide, quill, bone, metal
Knife: Length 13½
Sheath: Length 9
Cat. no. 50.67.59
Collected by N. S. Jarvis near Fort Snelling, 1833-36.

Buffalo Bill Historical Center, Cody, Wyoming

Flintlock Gun, English
Metal, wood
Length 57½
Cat. no. 78.1.2961
From the original Winchester firearm collection, New Haven, Connecticut.

Dog Travois, Northern Plains
Wood, hide
Length 107
Cat. no. NA.403.56a,b

Chandler Institute, Mission, South Dakota

Bead Hanks (3)
Glass
Length 10
Italian manufacture, twentieth century.

Dentalium Shells (24)
Length ⅞

Whiskey Keg
Wood, metal
Height 12

Colorado Springs Fine Arts Center, Colorado Springs, Colorado

Blanket, Navajo
Wool
Length 54
Cat. no. TM 3696
Collected by A. Seligman in the late nineteenth or early twentieth century.

Denver Museum of Natural History, Denver, Colorado

Peace Medal, United States
Silver
Diameter 4
Cat. no. 10561
Thomas Jefferson medal, struck in 1801.

Deutsches Ledermuseum, Offenbach/Main, West Germany

Robe, Blackfeet
Hide, paint
Length 88½
Cat. no. 4.44.09
Collected by Maximilian.

Field Museum of Natural History, Chicago, Illinois

Buffalo Robe, Sioux
Hide, paint
Length 42
Cat. no. 12972
Collected by F. B. Mayer, 1851.

The InterNorth Art Foundation/Joslyn Art Museum, Omaha, Nebraska

Ammunition Pouch
Hide, fabric
Length 10
Originally the property of Maximilian.

Game Bag
Fiber, woven
Length 15
Originally the property of Maximilian.

Rifle
Metal, wood
Length 45
Originally the property of Maximilian.

Linden-Museum, Stuttgart, West Germany

Knife, German?
Metal, wood
Length 20½
Cat. no. 36-070
Originally the property of Maximilian.

War Emblems (7), Mandan
Wood, paint, metal
Length 9
Cat. no. 36-076-a-f
Collected by Maximilian from Mató-Tópe.

War Whistle, Mandan
Bone, hide, quills
Length 9
Cat. no. 36-082
Collected by Maximilian from Mató-Tópe.

Moccasins, Winnebago
Hide, beads
Length 11
Cat. no. 36-084
Collected by Maximilian.

Museum of the American Indian, Heye Foundation, New York, New York

Pipe Tomahawk
Wood, metal
Length 24
Cat. no. 3/6398

Pipe, Hidatsa/Mandan
Wood
Length 19¾
Cat. no. 7/8199
Collected by G. Wilson at Fort Berthold.

Leggings, Upper Missouri
Hide, beads, paint, cloth
Length 34
Cat. no. 8/8033
Collected by T. S. Twiss at Fort Laramie ca. 1850.

Headdress, Assiniboin Style
Antelope horn, hide, cloth, feathers, quills, beads, horsehair
Length 34½
Cat. no. 10/8301
From the N. Salsbury collection.

Dress, Upper Missouri
Hide, beads, cloth
Length 54
Cat. no. 10/8454
Collected by T. S. Twiss ca. 1860.

Knife, Blackfeet
Bone (bear jaw), hide, wood, metal
Length 14
Cat. no. 11/5086
Collected by W. Wildschut in 1922; originally the property of Spotted Bear.

Hoop and Pole Game, Crow
Wood, hide, feather
Hoop: Diameter 14
Poles: Length 52
Cat. no. 11/6603
Collected by W. Wildschut.

Shirt, Upper Missouri
Hide, quills, paint, hair
Length 31
Cat. no. 16/5277

Moccasins, Piegan Blackfeet
Hide, beads, quills, horsehair
Length 10½
Cat. no. 17/8027

Packet of Vermillion Paint Pigment, Chinese/Piegan Blackfeet
Paper, pigment
Length 2½
Cat. no. 22/1841
From the C. F. Schuster collection.

The Museum of the Fur Trade, Chadron, Nebraska

Arrowheads (2), Sioux
Metal
Length 3
Cat. nos. 2334 & 4295
From the Yanders and Chadron collections.

Flints (2), British
Stone
Length 1
Cat. no. T-2827a&b
From the F. T. Dexter collection.

Bullets (3)
Lead
28 guage
Cat. no. T-3795
Molded in 1950 in a ca. 1820 British trade bullet mold.

Tobacco Twist
Length 8
Twentieth century.

National Museum of Man, National Museums of Canada, Ottawa, Canada

Gunstock War Club, Upper Missouri
Wood, paint, metal
Length 29
Cat. no. V-N-3
Collected by Maximilian.

National Museum of Natural History, Smithsonian Institution, Washington, D.C.

Moccasin, Upper Missouri
Hide, beads, quills, cloth
Length 11
Cat. no. 1899
Collected by G. K. Warren.

Rattle, Sioux
Wood, hide, beads, dewclaws, metal
Length 14½
Cat. no. 1925
Collected by G. K. Warren.

Shield Cover, Upper Missouri
Hide, paint
Diameter 23
Cat. no. 2671
From the War Department collection.

Choker Necklace, Upper Missouri
Hide, beads, metal
Diameter 8
Cat. no. 5419
Collected by J. Varden ca. 1855.

Hair Pipes (2), Plains
Shell
Length 3
Cat. no. 115695

War Hatchet, Kansa
Wood, metal, cloth
Length 21¾
Cat. no. 127621
Collected by J. O. Dorsey at the Kaw Agency.

Ladle, Sioux
Horn
Length 20
Cat. no. 153937
From the M. M. Hazen collection.

Fan, Plains
Feather, fur
Length 23½
Cat. no. 272408
Collected by E. Wagner.

Pipe Tamper, Sioux
Wood, quills
Length 15½
Cat. no. 290385
From the C. E. Bates collection.

Rings (5), Plains
Copper
Diameter ¾
Cat. no. 395574
Collected by E. W. J. Lindesmith at Fort Keogh in 1907.

Shirt, Upper Missouri
Hide, paint, quills, hair
Length 36
Cat. no. 403344A

Hair Bow, Plains
Hide, beads
Length 4¼
Cat. no. T-1165

Bells (6), Plains
Brass
Diameter ½
Cat. no. T-14926

Nebraska State Historical Society, Lincoln, Nebraska

Earrings (4), Pawnee
Brass
Length 1½
Cat. no. 4360
From the J. R. Coffin collection; believed to have been the property of Petalasharo (d. 1874).

Staatliche Museen Preussischer Kulturbesitz, Museum für Völkerkunde, Berlin, West Germany

Basket, Cherokee
Splints
Diameter 7
Cat. no. IV-B-77
Collected by Maximilian.

Moccasin, Iroquois
Hide, quills
Length 8¾
Cat. no. IV-B-128b
Collected by Maximilian.

Snowshoe, Mandan
Wood, hide, cloth
Length 31
Cat. no. IV-B-144a
Collected by Maximilian.

Parfleche, Cheyenne/Sioux
Hide, paint
Width 16
Cat. no. IV-B-160
Collected by Maximilian.

Buffalo Robe, Piegan Blackfeet
Hide, paint, quills
Length 105½
Cat. no. IV-B-201
Collected by Maximilian.

Bow and Arrow, Sioux
Wood, paint, hide, feathers
Arrow: Length 30
Bow: Length 42
Cat. no. IV-B-264a,b
Collected by Maximilian.

The University Museum, University of Pennsylvania, Philadelphia, Pennsylvania

Leggings, Upper Missouri
Hide, quills, paint, beads, hair
Length 38½
Cat. no. 38251
From the T. Donaldson collection; possibly originally collected by G. Catlin.

Pipe Bowl, Sioux
Catlinite, lead
Length 5¼
Cat. no. 38380
From the T. Donaldson collection; possibly originally collected by G. Catlin.

Earrings, Northern Plains
Shell, beads, hide
Length 7
Cat. no. 45-15-562a,b
From the C. H. Stevens collection.

Buffalo Robe, Upper Missouri
Hide, quills
Length 100
Cat. no. 45-15-702
From the C. H. Stevens collection; believed to have been made by the Mandan wife of James Kipp.

Pipe Stem, Northern Plains
Wood, beads, metal, feathers, hide
Length 23½
Cat. no. 45-15-1374b
From the McClure and C. H. Stevens collections.

Earrings, Northern Plains
Shell, beads, hide
Length 5¼
Cat. no. 52-6-7a,b

Ring, Arapaho
Brass
Diameter 1
Cat. no. L-84-1905
From the collections of the Academy of Natural Sciences of Philadelphia.

NATURAL HISTORY SPECIMENS

All specimens are from the collections of the American Museum of Natural History, New York, New York, the Departments of Mammalogy, Herpetology and Ornithology.

Eutamias minimus pallidus
Ground squirrel
Cat. no. 781
Collected by Maximilian.

Lampropeltis getulus holbrooki
King snake
Cat. no. 3705
Collected by Maximilian.

Chrysemys picta
Painted turtle, juvenile
Cat. no. 7055
Collected by Maximilian.

Colaptes auratus
Yellow-shafted flicker, mounted

Richmondena cardinalis
Cardinal, mounted

Geothlypis trichas
Yellowthroat, skin
Cat. no. 384134

Gymnorhinus cyanocephala
Maximilian's jay, skin
Cat. no. 372716

DOCUMENTS AND OTHER ARCHIVAL MATERIAL

The InterNorth Art Foundation/Joslyn Art Museum, Omaha, Nebraska

MANUSCRIPT MATERIAL:

Journal, Volume 2 of Maximilian's three-volume account of his travels in North America in 1832-34.

Diary, Maximilian's account of the voyage from Europe to Boston. 1832.

Contract between Maximilian and Karl Bodmer for Bodmer's services. April 20, 1832.

Bill for board, lodging, supplies and services from Dr. Henry Woehler, Bethlehem, Pennsylvania. September 15, 1832.

Maps, thirty-nine sheets, copies of William Clark's original 1804-06 maps of the Missouri and Yellowstone Rivers, hand-traced or drawn for Maximilian. 1833.

Letter from Maximilian to his brother Karl, with drawing of Indian. November 18, 1833.

Account sheet for supplies provided to Maximilian by the American Fur Company at Fort Clark. November 1833-April 1834.

Letter from Karl Bodmer to Maximilian. March 1, 1837.

PRINTED MATTER:

Map of Pennsylvania, New Jersey and Delaware. Philadelphia: S. A. Mitchell, n.d.

Passport, Prussian, for Maximilian, Prince of Wied.

Advertisement for the New Harmony Drug and Chemical Store. New Harmony, 1828.

Broadside advertising the Mississippi-Ohio steamboat *Homer.* ca. 1830.

Broadside advertising Niagara Falls. ca. 1830.

Broadside advertising the Ohio steamboat *Wyoming.* ca. 1830.

A catalogue of drugs, dyestuffs, chemicals and miscellaneous articles from the Philadelphia firm of W. & L. Krumbhaar, Importers and Manufacturers. ca. 1830.

Broadside advertising the Philadelphia and Mauch Chunk line of post coaches. 1832.

Broadside advertising the steamboat *Yellow Stone.* St. Louis, 1832.

Electoral tickets for the presidential election (Henry Clay-President; John Sergeant-Vice-President). 1832.

Map of the State of Missouri and Territory of Arkansas. Philadelphia: S. A. Mitchell, 1832.

Bill for chemical supplies from Place and Souillard, New York City. July 11, 1832.

Invitation to Christmas ball at the New Harmony Hotel. 1832.

Invitation to celebration ball at the Layfayette Hotel in New Harmony. 1833.

Advertisement for theatre performance, city unknown. 1834.

Bill for board and lodging from the Eagle Hotel, Niagara Falls. July 1, 1834.

BOOKS:

Maximilian, Prince of Wied. *Travels in Brazil in the Years 1815, 1816, 1817.* London: H. Colburn, 1820.

Maximilian, Prince of Wied. *Reise nach Brasilie in den Jahren 1815 bis 1817.* Frankfurt: H. L. Brönner, 1821.

Companion to Mitchell's Traveller's Guide Through the United States. Philadelphia: Mitchell & Hinman, 1834.

Maximilian, Prince of Wied. *Reise in das Innere Nord-America in den Jahren 1832 bis 1834.* Koblenz: J. Hoelscher, 1839-41.

Print Collection, The New York Public Library, Astor, Lenox and Tilden Foundations, New York City

Sketch of Karl Bodmer
Jean-Francois Millet
Photoreproduction

Lenders to the Exhibition

American Museum of Natural History
New York, New York

The Brooklyn Museum
Brooklyn, New York

Buffalo Bill Historical Center
Cody, Wyoming

Chandler Institute
Mission, South Dakota

Colorado Springs Fine Arts Center
Colorado Springs, Colorado

Denver Museum of Natural History
Denver, Colorado

Deutsches Ledermuseum
Offenbach/Main, West Germany

Field Museum of Natural History
Chicago, Illinois

Linden-Museum
Stuttgart, West Germany

Museum of the American Indian, Heye Foundation
New York, New York

The Museum of the Fur Trade
Chadron, Nebraska

National Museum of Man, National Museums of Canada
Ottawa, Canada

National Museum of Natural History, Smithsonian Institution
Washington, D.C.

Nebraska State Historical Society
Lincoln, Nebraska

The New York Public Library, Astor, Lenox and Tilden Foundations
New York, New York

Staatliche Museen Preussischer Kulturbesitz, Museum für Völkerkunde
Berlin, West Germany

The University Museum, University of Pennsylvania
Philadelphia, Pennsylvania

Acknowledgments

In appreciation of their generous support of *Views of a Vanishing Frontier,* I wish to thank W.A. Strauss, Chairman of the Board of InterNorth, Inc., and Sam F. Segnar, President and Chief Executive Officer.

I would also like to express my thanks to James J. Finnegan, Executive Director of the InterNorth Art Foundation, and to Dorothy McCormick, Assistant Director, for their significant assistance with the exhibition.

My special thanks to Richard R. Lynes, Manager of Corporate Public Relations, InterNorth, and Peter S. Bradley, Senior Vice President, Bozell and Jacobs, for the assistance provided in the development of the public relations program.

For their participation with the tour of the show, I particularly want to acknowledge Jan K. Muhlert, Director, Amon Carter Museum; Ian M. White, Director, The Fine Arts Museums of San Francisco, M.H. de Young Memorial Museum; Richard S. Fiske, Director, National Museum of Natural History, Smithsonian Institution; and Philippe de Montebello, Director, The Metropolitan Museum of Art, whose institution is presenting a selection of the Bodmer watercolors.

Among those responsible for the organization and content of this exhibition were members of the staff of the Joslyn Art Museum's Center for Western Studies including Marsha V. Gallagher, Curator of Material Culture; David C. Hunt, Curator of Western American Art; William J. Orr, Curator of Manuscripts; Joseph C. Porter, Curator of Western American History and Ethnology; and Marilyn Shanewise, Administrative Assistant. Other Joslyn staff members deserving recognition for their special contributions to the project are: Theodore W. James, Associate Director for Art; Audrey S. Kauders, Associate Director for Administration; Anne El-Omami, Curator of Education; Janice J. Braden, Special Events Coordinator; Allison C. Perkins, Volunteer Coordinator; Edward Quick, Head of Registration and Preparation; Berneal Anderson, Registrar; Michael A. Tegland, Preparator; Ann E. Birney, Art Librarian; and Marie Sedlacek, Library Cataloguer.

John C. Ewers, Ethnologist Emeritus, Smithsonian Institution, served as ethnographic consultant to the exhibition and also contributed the principle essay to this catalogue.

Deserving special acknowledgment for the design of the exhibition is the firm of Staples & Charles Ltd, Washington, D.C.

Others who have contributed to the preparation of this exhibition and catalogue are Malcolm Varon, Photographer, New York; Lorran Meares, Photographer, Bristol, Virginia; D.A. Saunders, Chief Naturalist, Fontenelle Forest Nature Center, Bellevue, Nebraska; and Jean Evans, Photographic Colorist, Omaha, Nebraska.

Many individuals from museums in North America and Europe were of assistance to us during the organization of this exhibition. These include the following:

American Museum of Natural History: Thomas D. Nicholson, Director; Stanley Freed, Curator, North American Ethnology; Barbara Conklin, Registrar of Collections, Department of Anthropology; Belinda Kaye, Archivist, Department of Anthropology; Anibal Rodriguez, Curatorial Assistant, Department of Anthropology; Charles W. Myers, Chairman and Curator, Department of Herpetology; George Foley, Senior Technician; Guy G. Musser, Chairman and Curator, Department of Mammalogy;

Daniel H. Russell, Curatorial Assistant; Wolfgang Fuchs, Curatorial Assistant; Lester L. Short, Chairman and Curator, Department of Ornithology; and Mary LeCroy, Scientific Assistant, Department of Ornithology.

The Brooklyn Museum: Robert Buck, Director; Diana Fane, Associate Curator in Charge, Department of African, Oceanic and New World Cultures; and Barbara LaSalle, Registrar.

Buffalo Bill Historical Center: Peter H. Hassrick, Director; George P. Horse Capture, Curator, Plains Indian Museum; and Debbi A. Stambaugh, Registrar.

Chandler Institute: F. Dennis Lessard, Director.

Colorado Springs Fine Arts Center: Paul Piazza, Director; Jonathan Batkin, Acting Curator of the Taylor Museum; and Laura B. Hoge, Registrar.

Denver Museum of Natural History: Charles T. Crockett, Director; Joyce Herold, Chief Curator and Curator of Anthropology; Robert Akerley, Assistant Curator of Anthropology; Barbara Stone, Collections Manager; and Elizabeth Clancy, Registrar.

Field Museum of Natural History: Lorin I. Nevling, Jr., Director; James W. Van Stone, Curator of North American Archaeology and Ethnology; Phyllis Rabineau, Custodian of Collections; and Terry Novak, Anthropology Registrar.

Museum of the American Indian, Heye Foundation: Roland Force, Director; James G.E. Smith, Curator of North American Ethnology; Gary Galante, Assistant Curator, Department of North American Ethnology; David Fawcett, Registrar; and Lisa Callendar, Assistant Registrar.

The Museum of the Fur Trade: Charles E. Hanson, Jr., Director.

National Museum of Natural History, Smithsonian Institution: Richard S. Fiske, Director; Douglas H. Ubelaker, Chairman, Department of Anthropology; William L. Merrill, Associate Curator, Department of Anthropology; Bruce Craig, Loan Coordinator, Department of Anthropology; Margaret Lethbridge, Museum Technician, Department of Anthropology; and Jane Norman, Conservator.

Nebraska State Historical Society: Marvin F. Kivett, Director; Wendell Frantz, Curator of Lincoln Museum; and Gail DeBuse Potter, Curator of Decorative Arts.

The New York Public Library, Astor, Lenox and Tilden Foundations: Donald Anderle, Associate Director for Special Collections.

The University Museum, University of Pennsylvania: Robert H. Dyson, Jr., Director; Gregory L. Possehl, Associate Director; Pamela Hearne, Keeper of the American Section; Virginia Greene, Conservator; Irene B. Romano, Acting Registrar; and Kathryn Grabowski, Assistant, Registrar's Office.

National Museum of Man, National Museums of Canada: W.E. Taylor, Jr., Director; Ted J. Brasser, Plains Ethnologist, Canadian Ethnology Service; Kathleen Bishop-Glover, Acting Curator of Collections, Canadian Ethnology Service; Judy Hall, Collection Researcher, Canadian Ethnology Service; and Marjorie E. Stanton, Registrar, Travelling Exhibitions.

Deutsches Ledermuseum: Günter Gall, Director; and Renate Wente-Lukas, Curator of Anthropology.

Linden-Museum Stuttgart: Friedrich Kussmaul, Director; and Axel Schulze-Thulin, Curator, American Department.

Staatliche Museen Preussischer Kulturbesitz, Museum für Völkerkunde: Dr. Wolf-Dieter Dube, General Director; Kurt Krieger, Director; Horst Hartmann, Curator; and Peter Thiele, Curator, East Asia Department.

Henry Flood Robert, Jr.
Director, Joslyn Art Museum

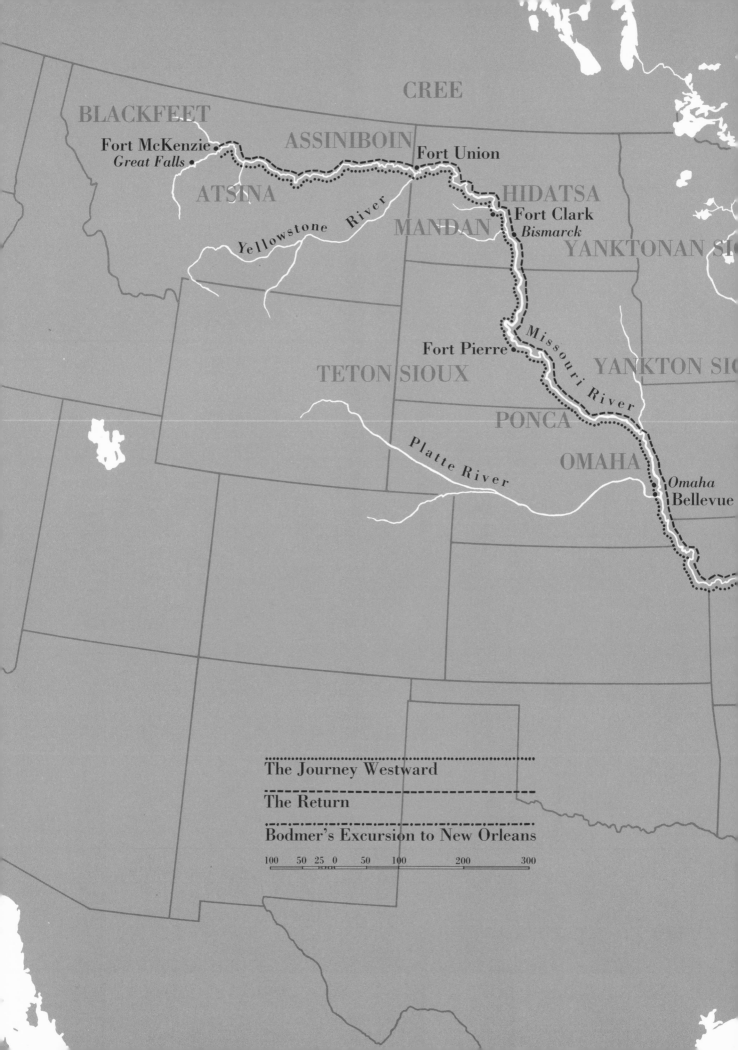

CREE

BLACKFEET

Fort McKenzie •
Great Falls •

ASSINIBOIN

Fort Union

ATSINA

Yellowstone River

HIDATSA

Fort Clark
Bismarck •

MANDAN

YANKTONAN SI

Fort Pierre •

Missouri River

TETON SIOUX

YANKTON SI

PONCA

Platte River

OMAHA

Omaha
Bellevue

•••••••••• The Journey Westward

– – – – The Return

–·–·–· Bodmer's Excursion to New Orleans

100   50 25 0   50   100   200   300